BOOK LOVE

Developing Depth, Stamina, and Passion in Adolescent Readers

Penny Kittle

HEINEMANN
Portsmouth, NH

Heinemann
361 Hanover Street
Portsmouth, NH 03801–3912
www.heinemann.com

Offices and agents throughout the world

The author and publisher wish to thank those who have generously given permission to reprint borrowed material:

"Where Dreams Come From" from *The Hunger Moon: New and Selected Poems* by Marge Piercy. Copyright © 2011 by Middlemarsh, Inc. Used by permission of Alfred A. Knopf, a division of Random House, Inc.

Acknowledgments for borrowed material continue on page xvii.

Library of Congress Cataloging-in-Publication Data
Kittle, Penny.
    Book love : developing depth, stamina, and passion in adolescent readers / Penny Kittle.
        p. cm.
    Includes bibliographical references.
    ISBN-13: 978-0-325-04295-4
    ISBN-10: 0-325-04295-0
    1. Reading (Secondary).   2. Teenagers—Books and reading.   I. Title.
LB1632.K54 2013
428.4071'2—dc23   2012029994

Editor: Anita Gildea
Consulting editor: Tom Newkirk
Production: Vicki Kasabian
Cover and interior designs: Monica Ann Crigler
Cover and interior photos: Kori Sandman and Samantha Forde
Typesetter: Gina Poirier
Manufacturing: Steve Bernier

Printed in the United States of America on acid-free paper
21 20 19 18 17   VP   6 7 8 9 10

To my mom, Barbara Ostrem,
who led me to love reading so much,
I had to pass it on.

The Beatles might have thought that all you need is love, but lucky for teachers, Penny Kittle knows better. She knows that when you want to create lifetime readers, you not only need to fill the room with books, not only need to show your own passion about books, but you also need to help kids develop lifetime reading habits. In this book, Penny shows all of us how to help kids develop those habits as she shares masterful teaching strategies that turn aliterate students who can read into those who want *to* read.

—**Kylene Beers,** author of *When Kids Can't Read—What Teachers Can Do*
and coauthor of *Notice and Note*

Book Love is nothing short of miraculous. Penny Kittle knows the developmental stage of adolescence like she invented it. This book alone could make me a good teacher. It's detailed, so incredibly readable, and, I swear, filled with simple miracles.

—**Chris Crutcher,** author of *Period 8*

When Penny Kittle says, "We can't wait for someone else to teach our students to love books," she understands that raising students who love books is much more important than raising students who become good test takers or who "fake read" their way to good grades. With this in mind, Kittle's Book Love focuses on a critical question all but forgotten in this age of standards and testing: What can we, as teachers, do to help our students develop a love for reading? Book Love is a breath of fresh air. It challenges many damaging practices that have become norms in our nation's classrooms, offering insightful, practical ways for teachers to begin instilling a love of reading in our students and showing teachers and administrators how to build reading lives that last. Kittle is right—we cannot wait for someone else to teach our students to love reading. It starts with us, and I am hopeful that for many teachers it will start with this book.

—**Kelly Gallagher,** author of *Readicide*

Worried the teenagers you teach will never pick up a book on their own? Let Penny Kittle show you how to kindle a passion for reading with authentic texts and techniques aimed at students' most vulnerable spot—their hearts.

—**Carol Jago,** past president, National Council of Teachers of English,
and author of *With Rigor for All*

How many times can you fall in love? By reading, you can fall in love every time you begin a new book or reread a treasured one. In Book Love, Penny Kittle invites us into her high school classroom where many of her students fall in love with reading for the first time. Through reading research, her practical classroom rituals, and the powerful words of her students as they describe years spent not reading much, Penny builds an undeniable case for pleasure reading in the high school English classroom as a path to reading competence, stamina, and engagement.

—**Donalyn Miller,** author of *The Book Whisperer*

Where Dreams Come From

A girl slams the door of her little room
under the eaves where marauding squirrels
scamper overhead like herds of ideas.
She has forgotten to be grateful she has
finally a room with a door that shuts.

She is furious her parents don't comprehend
why she wants to go to college, that place
of musical comedy fantasies and weekend
football her father watches, beer can
in hand. It is as if she announced I want
to journey to Iceland or Machu Picchu.
Nobody in their family goes to college.
Where do dreams come from? Do they
sneak in through torn screens at night
to light on the arm like mosquitoes?

Are they passed from mouth to ear
like gossip or dirty jokes? Do they
sprout from underground on damp
mornings like toadstools that form
fairy rings on dewtipped grasses?

No, they slink out of books, they lurk
in the stacks of libraries. Out of pages
turned they rise like the scent of peonies
and infect the brain with their promise.
I want, I will, says the girl and already

she is halfway out the door and down
the street from this neighborhood, this
mortgaged house, this family tight
and constricting as the collar on the next
door dog who howls on his chain all night.

—Marge Piercy

Contents

Reading should not be presented to a child as a chore, a duty.
It should be offered as a gift.

—Kate DiCamillo

Acknowledgments

My heartfelt thanks to . . .

Thanks to teachers who believed in my insolent self, the 4:30 alarm even in January, and especially Pat, who said one evening, "Is all of that movie making distracting you from getting your book written?" Yes, I made this face, but I needed to hear it.

I am continually inspired by the wonder, the magic, and the heart-stopping joy of books!

Thanks to Kennett students Samantha Forde and Kori Sandman for running lively and joyful photo shoots (and Theresa Sires for your expertise) and all of the Conway School District colleagues and students who read, think, and write with me. To Jack Loynd, Neal Moylan, and Kevin Richard: you are leaders to believe in.

There are so many of you who help me live in joy and wonder. . . . First of all, the family at Heinemann. Where would I be without you? Huge thanks for clarity and vision to my editor, mentor, visionary, and friend: Tom Newkirk. Also to Lesa Scott, who holds us together, and to Anita Gildea, who is a compassionate and wise guide. To Sarah Fournier in editorial, Monica Crigler in design, Alan Huisman in editing, Kim Cahill in marketing, and Vicki Kasabian in production: you have made this a better book. I am truly grateful. To former editors Lois Bridges and Lisa Luedeke: you made me believe in one word and then the next. And to Michelle Flynn and Cheryl Savage who keep my traveling life sane: bless you.

I am a better teacher and writer because of the warmth and guidance of friends who are not only wicked smart, they help me see the magic in living, laughing, and writing: Tom Romano, Kelly Gallagher, Maja Wilson, Linda Rief, Matt Glover, Jim Burke, Ed Fayle, Stevi Quate, Karen Hartman, Kylene Beers, and Bob Probst. To Donalyn Miller and Franki Sibberson—thanks for the late-night writing chat in the midst of winter. And to Ann Carboneau—you know why.

My life was changed when two men, Don Graves and Don Murray, invited me into a community of writers. I still write beside them.

To Pat, Cam, and Hannah . . . I love books, but I love you more. Now let's get back to fun!

Thanks to YOU who have listened to me work out my thinking in workshops over the last several years and to those who have written me notes: your belief in the power of teaching is all over my work.

Introduction

This is a love story.

It began on Belmont Street in a small back room painted a spunky pink. My mother held a collection of *Winnie-the-Pooh* stories across her lap as her two daughters eagerly awaited the reading. I was the younger one—blonde pixie haircut, chubby hands clapping gleefully, "Let's go, Mom!" I can still close my eyes and walk in those imagined woods.

Mom led me through the Laura Ingalls Wilder books until I could navigate them on my own. I read my way through the Montavilla Public Library, challenging myself, rereading favorites, learning to discriminate and refine my tastes. I read everything my favorite authors wrote. (Still do.) I picked strawberries and hosted the neighborhood lemonade stand with my best friend to buy books until the shelf above my bed began to sag with *Encyclopedia Brown*, *Harriet the Spy*, *The Hobbit*, and on to *The Lord of the Rings*. Faithful friends—they carried me joyfully through middle school.

I entered honors English in ninth grade at age thirteen, sure of my success. A serious and soft-spoken man stood behind the wooden lectern he gripped with both hands and told us how good the books were: *Pride and Prejudice*, *The Scarlet Letter*, *Macbeth*. It was dull and lifeless in that small room on the first floor where I counted the dust-smothered blades of the window blinds to keep awake. I didn't read more than a few pages each night. I would grab my basketball and play until dark. I was good at half-listening to lectures, so I collected my As each quarter and moved on, but I don't have a single memory of joy during high school English. Perhaps this book love was only for children. I almost believed it.

In college I majored in elementary education. I read books like the last deep breath you take before a dive. In philosophy, psychology, political science, Western civilization, and oceanography I found that all I knew was a small part of all I might know if I kept reading. I was invigorated by the challenge. I powered through books for my English minor: poetry, Shakespeare, British literature, American drama, protest essays for the honors program, and, again, stories whose characters walked beside me on my way to class. I *loved* those books. I will never forget my first Henry James, my first Tolstoy, my first Brontë. And yes, my first Jane Austen. Small wonder I eventually ended up as a high school English teacher.

But suddenly it was all too familiar: the slouching students, the yellowed pages of novels they weren't reading, the "doing time" feel to the curriculum assigned to me. Surely my ineptitude contributed to the lack of engagement I faced, but my classes were also filled with students I didn't recognize from high school: students who could barely read, who had no memories of book love to carry them through the dull parts in a play or a line that confused them in a poem. Students who had never been read to. Students who told me reading just wasn't for them. Nice students, not defiant, just not interested. I tried to listen to my department chair, but she told me students were lazy and I should give them a reading quiz each day to *make* them read. Quizzes don't make people read, and besides, teaching isn't police work; I *knew* this. I wanted to be a master sorcerer and entice all students into deep reading; she wanted to set traps to catch criminals. She snorted at my literature circles and my attempts to bring other authors into the room. My throat tightened. I stopped visiting the department office, secluded myself in a corner of the building, and turned my attention to my students. Because here's the other side of this love story: the kids.

I didn't enter the field of English teaching only because of my passion for words but also because of my deep belief in the power of an education to transform a life. Mine. Theirs. I worked with all levels of students but always sought those who struggled, those potential first-generation-to-go-to-college students I saw almost reaching for what felt beyond them. I loved the challenge and the joy of leading them. And those kids needed a bridge. Many had read in elementary school, and a few continued into middle school, but almost none were reading now. I knew they would never succeed in college without the stamina to read hundreds of pages a week. More important, they needed to reexperience the power of books. The books I grew to love in college were not the answer. Not yet. Maybe not ever. First I had to lead them back to reading. Perhaps then I could entice them into the great, lasting literature I wanted all kids to know. I knew if I could figure out the pedagogy of increasing complexity *and* passion, I would never fall out of love with teaching. So with no support and without permission but with great determination and a fierce love, I turned my attention from content to kids and began again.

I asked myself, what if I took my department's mission seriously—to create readers and writers for life? Was it even possible with kids today? Could I do it? Could I sustain it? Could I lead my students to literature?

I could. I did. This book tells that story.

I believe in the rigor of independent reading. I believe in the power of guiding student choice to increase engagement, skill, and joy. It is a pedagogy well defined by teachers who've written about their work—Nancie Atwell, Linda Rief, Donalyn Miller—but often dismissed by high school teachers as a pedagogy for middle school, since all the women I just mentioned teach middle school students. It isn't. It is for *all* readers. At its core is the belief that we are launching readers for life—into life—and that although reading more will have an important impact on SAT and ACT scores and on preparing students for the volume of reading in college, it also enlarges their worldview and gives them a greater understanding of the complexities of arguments so often truncated on the news. Independence is indispensable in life, and it is at the center of what the Common Core State Standards seek for all readers, K–12. Independence—the act of reading deeply and engaging critically with a text—depends on thinking. Rigorous independent reading will not only build background knowledge and vocabulary but also provide a fundamental necessity: regular practice. Teachers must create a love for books that will drive students to reach for them every school year.

Allowing students to make choices about what they read has been presented in our profession, especially at the secondary level, as enrichment—something to do once the hard work is over. I believe, instead, that it is at the center of our work. We have to teach some students how to slow down and enjoy the rhythm of story. We invite others into a community of readers who are idiosyncratic but purposeful. Students need a vast knowledge of text types, far more than we teach in the traditional English curriculum, precisely because of the increased complexity of literacy in this age; yet we all know students who shun books and most lengthy texts. They need to read more than ever, yet most secondary students rebel against whole-class reading in English class. What to do? I believe all students need to own their reading in the same way I believe they must own their writing.

Wise teachers can place literature within reach of any student, but without the stamina to read long and well, students will abandon it. Instead of leading students to independence, we make them dependent on us. Or worse, we teach them *not* to rely on us because we so often pick books they don't connect with. Without regular practice with whole books and the endurance to read them, students will be unable to overcome the confusion in classic literature that defeats them. They don't hunger for meaning, so they hunger for shortcuts. I believe in a marriage of two approaches—directly teaching vivid, short texts and a few whole-class novels, coupled with intentionally cultivating a reading life of increased volume, complexity, and pleasure. Whole-class novels are still important but less so. This is an active environment, not an open library for casual reading. There is nothing casual here. Understanding the habits, interests, and challenges of individual readers becomes a central part of teaching. This reading-life pedagogy elevates the role of conferences. We have to pull in close to our readers and listen. This pedagogy requires all we have, but it engages all kids, and that is always worth fighting for.

The thinking here is for your students. Even in schools where test scores are high and funds are plentiful, the hunger to read is too often absent in courses at all levels. I've learned this from listening. A friend who has taught English in an exclusive private school for thirty years told me last summer, "I can't get my students to read novels anymore. I *know* almost all of them aren't reading." At an international school where I spent two inspiring weeks working beside students and teachers this year, a student responded to my question, "Do you think there are kids here fake-reading?" with a laugh. "Of course! People say it all the time: I got an A on that quiz or paper and I didn't even read the book."

Where is the hunger? We must cultivate it. I know it when I see it. Matt bursts into my room on a mild May morning shouting, "Mrs. Kittle! There are 'answers to questions I didn't even know I was asking' in here—there are!" His joy at quoting my assurance that all of us can find books just for us is palpable. It has taken until May of senior year, but he's found one. We must keep fighting for that moment. We must connect students to books that force them to pay attention, to think and wonder, to imagine and believe, and then to read for the rest of their lives.

Our beliefs as teachers impact our practice, as Samantha Bennett and Cris Tovani have wisely noted. Do we believe kids today are too busy to read? It's simply not true. Have your colleagues told you that kids will cheat, even when given choice? They're wrong. Kids show me again and again that they'll find time to read if given books that name what's in their hearts. But it is also true that given access to a wide variety of books, they will choose challenging ones as they develop confidence and are introduced to the array of truly stunning works of literature produced every year across the world. Spend time with kids and books they want to read and you will be a believer.

The great voices of centuries past are still relevant today, but too often we haven't convinced most students this is true. We can't give up and accept so few readers. We also can't have every student start with Austen, no matter what the Common Core or your department chair says. A book isn't rigorous if students aren't reading it. Every student must become a reader who *can* read Jane Austen. How? We start where they are. We start with an entry to a reading life and engagement with whole books, even if we feel they are less worthy than the classics. Yes, even *Twilight*, if that's the book that will get a student reading. Once students are reading regularly, voraciously, we can lead them further. Once students develop a loyalty to books and authors, creating identities as readers, they will move toward challenge. It happens every year in my classroom; as I challenge my students, they read more. They also read more difficult texts. They learn to navigate hundreds of pages independently, and they amaze themselves with their willingness to find time for reading in the rush of life. Student stories, like the ones I'll share here with you, continue to energize and challenge me.

Driving home from teaching at the University of New Hampshire one day last summer, as I waited at a red light, I noticed a former student perched on the bumper of an old pickup truck parked just off the road. The truck was loaded with fresh corn on the cob, and I grinned at the homemade sign: *Six ears = $1*. Ah, sweet summer.

Just before the light turned green I glanced again at Cassie, lit by late afternoon sunlight. She was perfectly still, curled around a paperback she cradled in her right hand. Traffic started up again, tourists honked and lunged forward, but Cassie didn't even glance up. Perhaps she was walking with the Lost Boys of Sudan or spinning across the stage as a ballerina. There are endless possibilities, we know, even for a student not going to college. I want readers seeking them for the rest of their lives. I work every day to make that happen in my classroom, and this book will show you how.

Acknowledgments continued from copyright page:

Excerpt from *The Other Wes Moore: One Name, Two Fates* by Wes Moore. Copyright © 2010 by Wes Moore. Used by permission of Spiegel & Grau, an imprint of the Random House Publishing Group, a division of Random House, Inc.

Excerpt from "What *Should* Kids Be Reading?" by Ellen Hopkins in the report *What Kids Are Reading, 2012*: http://www.renlearn.com/whatkidsarereading/. Used by permission of Renaissance Learning, Wisconsin Rapids, WI.

Excerpt from *Why We Broke Up* written by Daniel Handler with art by Maira Kalman. Text copyright © 2011 by Daniel Handler. Artwork copyright © 2011 by Maira Kalman. Published by Little, Brown and Company and Electric Monkey, an imprint of Egmont UK Ltd London. Used by permission of the publishers.

Excerpt from *Winter's Bone* by Daniel Woodrell. Copyright © 2006 by Daniel Woodrell. Used by permission of Little, Brown and Company and Hodder Stoughton Limited. All rights reserved.

Teenagers Want to Read—
If We Let Them

"Children want to write." These words are just as true now as they were
twenty years ago when I first wrote them, at the beginning of Chapter 1.
I would only add, "If we let them."

—**Donald H. Graves, in the preface to the twentieth anniversary edition of**
Writing: Teachers and Children at Work

Don Graves and I were good friends in the dozen years before his death. I cherish
the afternoons we spent on his deck eating graham crackers and talking about
reading, writing, and life. His impact on my thinking is immeasurable. I read Don's
seminal book on teaching writing as a new elementary teacher in 1984. The opening
line had been my mantra: children want to write. I planned my instruction to intersect
with student interests, knowing that captivating them was the first step in teaching
them. Don asked me to read a draft of the preface for the twentieth anniversary edition of the book, a book that had changed my teaching life, and I loved his addition
of "if we let them." One of Don's strengths was his ability to clarify succinctly what
teaching can and should be.

I have come to believe this same truth about reading. Teenagers want to read—if
we let them. Students who I believe are determined nonreaders become committed,
passionate readers given the right books, time to read, and regular responses to their
thinking. The pathway to difficult reading begins with books they enjoy. Once they're
reading, together we can reach for the challenging literature I want them to know.
Rich and rewarding reading lives are within reach for all of our students.

Even the boys I find *not* reading one morning in a colleague's mixed-grade reading break—twenty minutes every day when the entire school stills to silence (see
p. 141). The goal is to get all kids reading, and that's an immense challenge. We've

got more kids reading than ever, but I am always on the hunt for kids who don't read. Today I've got three.

You know these boys. We'll call them Tom and Allen and Patrick. Tom and Allen are slumped at the back of the room to my left; Patrick is to my right, just out of the teacher's sight, crouched behind a yellowed copy of *Frankenstein*. He shelters his phone in his hands as he reads the screen, texts, smiles.

Tom and Allen pull out identical permabound copies of *Fahrenheit 451* from their backpacks and spend the next twenty minutes not reading. Allen makes a show of compliance, studying a two-page spread for several minutes before dropping his head to his desk for several more. The pages never turn in that long, silent stretch of time. Tom stops to rub his eyes, pulls the book closer for a minute, then lets it flop to the desk. He kicks the chair of the kid in front of him, lets out a loud cough, then a sigh, looks at the book again for a minute, then bangs his forehead against the desk silently.

The ten other the kids in the room are deeply reading. There is a wide mixture of titles, and if you find yourself dismissing Jeremy because he's reading Harry Potter and not *The Brothers Karamazov*, well, I have to press you on that. Is reading really only about what's hard? Is there no place in school for what brings joy and escape and urges you to read to the end just to see how it all works out? Jeremy is one of my seniors. He lost both parents as a small child and is being raised by grandparents. He told me Harry Potter gives him hope that he will overcome his own isolation and sorrow. Would you still say there's no room for this reading in school? Because if school reading is only like boot camp, we lose readers. And I'm not just talking about dropouts. I'm talking about thousands of kids who survive English class with SparkNotes and skim the surface of their content classes, reading next to nothing that is assigned to them in four years. The recent addition of a reading break at our high school has helped our students find time for pleasure reading as well as textbook reading. Our school is richer for it. The kids certainly are. But a love of reading also has to be cultivated in regular English classes. Readers need attention, encouragement, and challenge. English teachers know how to provide all three.

Pleasure reading has suffered under the assessment mania of the last decade in the United States. Carol Gordon and Ya-Ling Lu (2007) report that "all adolescents are reading less. There is a downward trend in voluntary reading by youth at middle and high school levels over the past two decades." A National Endowment for the Arts report (2007) documented a downward trend in reading among secondary-school-age students since 1992: less than one third of thirteen-year-olds are daily readers, and fifteen- to twenty-four-year-olds spend only seven to ten minutes per day on voluntary reading, which is about 60 percent less time than the average American. Even in Ontario, Canada, according to the province's Education Quality and Accountability Office (2011), pleasure reading has declined: "Since 1998/99, the percentage of students in grade 3 who report they like to read has declined by almost a third, from 76% in 98/99 to only 50% in 2010/11. There has been a similar decline for grade 6 students, from 65% in 98/99 to 50% in 2010/11" (1). The way forward is to make people see themselves as participants in a community that views reading as a significant and enjoyable activity (Strommen and Mates 2004).

It is the way forward, but we know the enormity of the challenge.

I awake at four the next morning thinking about those boys I watched pretending to read. We know that many students read below grade level, but sometimes we ignore that fact and teach what we expect they should be able to read or what the curriculum says they must read. What is the cost? We don't talk about this enough—how what happens in seventh or tenth grade affects what our colleagues are able to do in twelfth and what the student will be able to read in college and beyond. Does our approach to teaching reading distance too many kids from books?

During a class break that morning I ask a tenth-grade English teacher, "What do we do for kids who can't or won't read *Fahrenheit 451*?" Not reading is a typical response when a student is outmatched by or uninterested in a text. Sure, they may discuss some big ideas of the book in class, but they don't become better readers when they don't read:

> *If students do not read the assigned texts, nothing important is happening in your literature classroom*—nothing very important to develop your students' reading and interpretive abilities is happening, no matter how many lectures you deliver, vocabulary words students "learn," elements of fiction students define, quizzes students take, essay test answers students write, or films you show. Nothing important is happening because student development of reading and interpretive abilities requires engaged reading. (Broz 2011, 15)

The teacher I'm talking to may not know this. She is a capable and committed professional, but she may think knowing about the books, not reading them, is enough. Or the best she can do. She cares about her students and literature, which is why I risk the question.

Her eyes register alarm. "What do you mean can't read it? They're in tenth grade."

I nod. "I know. But you know some kids can't read at grade level."

She hesitates. "Then they shouldn't be in the class." And that's not her complete answer, but we're between classes in the busyness of the hallway and this is not the time to dig in.

I send her an email later assuring her I know she's working hard and I'm just trying to uncover some answers for myself. She comes to my room after school with a list of projects students can do related to the book, differentiated by interest and perceived talent or learning style. She says, "They can choose any of these projects to show they understand." She's smart to have this list, because differentiation is the word of the year at our school and she'll be asked how she's differentiating. "They can make a CD cover"—she shows me, and then details ten other creative options.

I tell her this isn't what I'm asking. Students can get the gist of the book and give it back to us by listening in class, but do they leave tenth grade as stronger, more capable independent readers or just knowing the gist of a few books? Because knowing the gist is not going to lead students to deeper reading and empathy for people in our world or prepare them for independent reading in college or the workplace. "I think we have to pay attention to the readers *and* the books," I say.

She presses me. "There's nothing wrong with reading some things that are too hard for you. I did that in high school. There's nothing wrong with struggling." She's right. I sweated through Maryanne Wolf's *Proust and the Squid* last month—all those diagrams of the brain and words (*splenium, angular gyrus*) I became familiar with but never owned, never understood well enough. It was slow and difficult reading and I learned a lot. But (you knew this was coming) objection, Your Honor: all reading can't be hard. It's also good to sail through *Freedom,* by Jonathon Franzen, on the weekend, carried by the movie of the story, hundreds of pages in one big gulp

Think for a minute about how our brains work. The field of cognitive science has made discoveries in the last twenty-five years that can help us, but we rarely hear about them. A book I recommend is *Why Don't Students Like School? A Cognitive Scientist Answers Questions About How the Mind Works and What It Means for the Classroom,* by Daniel T. Willingham (2009). Brain science can help us understand the resistance students feel toward the study of literature and why I believe we must bridge this resistance with the deep and lasting value of reading books students choose. Willingham says, "It is self-defeating to give all of your students the same work. The less capable students will find it too difficult and will struggle against their brain's bias to mentally walk away from the schoolwork. To the extent that you can, it's smart, I think to assign work to individuals or groups of students that is appropriate to their current level of competence." Differentiation. We're expected to apply it to our work, but we aren't aware of the resources that will help us and—faced with large class sizes and rampant student disengagement—we are exhausted at the very idea. Nevertheless (and here's why I bring it up), "the fact is they are behind the others, and giving them work that is beyond them is unlikely to help them catch up, and is likely to make them fall still further behind" (22).

I ask you to read that quotation again, because it halts me every time. Our current practices in English classrooms may contribute to our students' lack of progress in reading. Willingham suggests that we are giving students work that is likely to make them "fall still further behind." When our curriculum is consistently too difficult for the readers we have, we'll send them on to our colleagues at the next grade level in a worse place than we received them. I wince at this. I know it's the truth, having taught seniors for twelve years now, but I blanch at the idea that some of my hardworking, determined colleagues are contributing to the lack of preparedness in my seniors and to their possible failure in college. It is one thing to say, "These kids aren't prepared." It's quite another to make them no better, or even worse, in the year that we have them.

This is what we know from our own experiences and from cognitive science: "We actually like to think. We are naturally curious, and we look for opportunities to engage in certain types of thought. But because thinking is so hard, the conditions have to be right for this curiosity to thrive, or we quit thinking rather readily" (9). This happens to me. I download a software program that comes with a manual. I am frustrated within the first few pages by how long the manual is—I don't want to read this—and how complicated it is—words and concepts I don't know or don't remember knowing—and how quickly I'm looking for an out. I'll just call Applecare and they'll tell me how to make it work, I think. If there were a SparkNotes for it, I'd find them.

When I interview Allen, who's on page 35 of *Fahrenheit 451*, he says he's read about five of those pages himself. He's following along in class, but the whole thing is just too confusing, he says. He thumbs through the remaining two-hundred-plus pages with a defeated sigh. You can read it in his face: there will be no joy here. He hasn't read in years. He's followed along each year as the class reads a few immensely difficult (to him) books, but the independent reading this more challenging text depends on has been entirely absent. Willingham says, "Working on problems that are of the right level of difficulty is rewarding, but working on problems that are too easy or too difficult is unpleasant" (13). Allen with his book, one complicated sentence after another, is me lifting weights that are too heavy in my Pilates class. I won't last long, and neither will he.

I believe this is about motivation, yes, and about an overtired, overtaxed brain. There's no pleasure in constant confusion, which is exactly the way Allen describes his reading to me. He doesn't have the capacity for frustration that he needs, gleaned from hours of reading practice, to understand much less enjoy this book. We need to see Allen as a reader who still needs instruction in reading. As Dav Pilkey (2012), author of many popular children's books, has said, "As adults, I think we sometimes forget how hard it is to learn to read. It's really, REALLY hard. If we add negative associations to something that is already difficult and often frustrating, we might just turn kids off of reading altogether, despite our best intentions" (28).

The good news: it is possible to increase Allen's interest and ability to read if we focus on building his capacity for reading. We can do this. First, we have to under-stand what to do and why. Allen needs to do a lot of reading to build his stamina for the next hard task. Independent reading is all about capacity building. But beware: some say when we give kids some choice about what they read, we've given up on our profession. They say teachers like me, who believe in young adult literature, just don't have the guts or the talent to make *The Great Gatsby* work for everyone. We can't let them bully us. They're wrong. Independent reading allows students to build stamina so they *can* read *Gatsby*. Pretending to read it is far more damaging. This is what I want for all students: the ability to read all kinds of books with understanding, including the literature in our cultural tradition.

I choose to build capacity rather than ignoring the truth that most kids don't— and many can't—read the novels in our curriculum. A system that supports volume helps adolescent brains develop structures for the problem solving necessary in more difficult reading. We give them the skills to pay attention as they read by helping them find books that are pleasurable for them, that invite them to attend. They will try because they want to understand terrorism in the Middle East or the life of an elephant scientist. They'll read slowly and puzzle out meanings and reread when they've lost the train of thinking because they want to know. They'll willingly practice the skills we desperately need them to develop because there is value to them in the knowledge they'll get from the effort. They need to practice those skills this year in my room and next year in yours. They need daily, sustained practice every year they are in school.

We know which students won't read each night for homework. As Anderson, Wilson, and Fielding (1988) found, struggling readers, the most in need of independent reading, simply do not read outside of school. We can say this isn't our fault because they arrived so far behind from where they should be, but if we don't do something to help them gain the skills they need for the rich, challenging texts we love, we are part of the problem. We can't send them on to our colleagues down the hall having made no progress, adding yet more frustrating, demoralizing reading experiences to their memory of English class. Too many students feel reading is hopeless (although they call it boring), and we've given them no reason to think otherwise.

As a K–12 literacy coach in my rural New Hampshire school district for the last twelve years, I've regularly traveled to five elementary schools and a middle school and spent part of each day at our high school teaching and listening to students. I know this much for sure: elementary school is most often a joyful place for reading and writing. There are exceptions, of course, but it is mostly true that the reading and writing workshops in which I have the privilege to work are filled with creation and challenge and exploration and thinking. And all students participate. The truth behind the "fourth-grade slump" is that reading becomes much harder as students get older; as Willingham says, "The amount of information you retain depends on the amount of information you already have" (34). We know that some students have limited experiences with books and words and places that foster thinking, like an art museum or a walk through the forest, and instead spend hours in passive activities like watching television shows or movies. This accumulation of experiences leads to the "Matthew effect" in literacy: the rich get richer and the poor get left behind (Stanovich 1986). So of course we see students in middle and high school struggling to comprehend without the background knowledge they need. Instead of steady growth toward reading proficiency, we see, as Dana Gioia wrote in the National Endowment for the Arts annual report on reading (2007), "The story the data tell is simple, consistent, and alarming. Although there has been measurable progress in recent years in reading ability at the elementary school level, all progress appears to halt as children enter their teenage years" (5).

It halts in our hands.

Dick Allington (2012) says reading lots at your reading level is what makes you a better reader—just like most things in life, actually. Take golf. When my son wanted to learn, we took him to par-three courses where Cam could score well before we took him to St. Andrews. If you want to cultivate a love of the game, you know you don't start with impossibly long fairways and slick greens that dip into shady sand traps. It won't take long to doubt your potential and give up if it's always hard. We've created that condition for too many readers in school. When do students read at grade level in high school? In middle school? Most of my colleagues say, "Not my job. I have curriculum to cover." I say, if not you, who?

I believe we own a reader's improvement in the year we have them. My colleague is responsible for making those three boys and all of the others on her class lists better readers. Reading only what is too hard and then telling them what it means is not making them better readers. They parrot what they heard in class, but they don't improve as readers. We have to change this dysfunctional relationship between readers and reading in adolescence. For me, that's about balance: our interests and theirs, rigor and ease. We must understand that reading at grade level in big gulps of hundreds of pages makes the hard reading possible. I'm making a case for literature that can and will be read by all if we first build bridges to get there. We need to redefine our mission as English teachers in an age when the Common Core State Standards call for reading a complexity of texts we know many of our students are not prepared to navigate. We're the ones doing the preparing, and we can do this work better.

This isn't about tenth grade; it is about readers. If we don't change something in high school, we send this student from there to a dorm room where he could have three hundred pages to read in one week after not reading much of anything in years. Unless we do more than parcel out truly difficult texts to nonreaders as they limp along reluctantly behind us, we've given up on their lives as readers. No one will care if Allen somehow remembers class discussions on Ray Bradbury if he can't read the nonfiction Pulitzer Prize–winning book assigned for freshman-year Development of

Western Civilization on his own, write about the ideas, and discuss them in class. That task will take stamina for reading, not just maturity. Failure in college is not only about responsibility (forgoing drinking for homework, for example): some kids are sent to college without the skills to make it. And we had years to teach them.

Readers need books that carry them along, compelling them to read. Readers need goals for the quarter, for the year, and we need to pay attention to quantity as well as quality in their reading lives. We can keep kids accountable with sustained pressure and encouragement, cultivating engagement with a wide variety of books. We've been flat-out wrong about nonreaders in middle and high school: they haven't forever missed their chance to fall in love with books. They will read. My students prove this every year.

We need to balance pleasure with challenge, increasing volume for all readers and setting up an environment in our classroom that manages kids as they choose books, set goals, and develop a reading habit. We have to consider how to teach reading skills through the deep analysis of texts, both short and long, and learn to confer with and assess readers in ways that will lead them toward more complex texts. Last, we have to have the courage to lead in our classrooms, in our schools, and in our communities as we commit to developing readers, writers, and thinkers who possess empathy and power. At the center of all this for me is a sign I read at the Save Our Schools March in Washington, D.C., in July 2011: *Nothing without joy.*

If you're like the me of ten years ago, with no chance of pulling my whole school together to stop the crimes occurring in our very halls, let alone swap class time for pleasure reading, and with only a paltry shelf of books purchased with my own money, you can still reconsider your role in building the reading lives of your students. You can dedicate yourself to all these kids who just don't know what they're missing.

Give the lasting gift of a reading life. After all, where would you be without it? And if not you, who?

An entry from my writing notebook that led to the section on page 16.

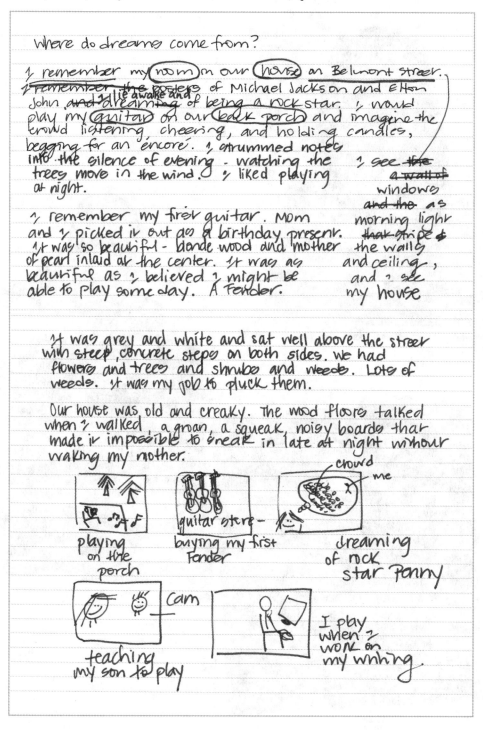

Where do dreams come from?

I remember my (mom) in our (house) on Belmont street. I remember the posters of Michael Jackson and Elton John. I lie awake and dreaming of being a rock star. I would play my (guitar) on our (back porch) and imagine the crowd listening, cheering, and holding candles, begging for an 'encore'. I strummed notes into the silence of evening. watching the trees move in the wind. I liked playing at night.

I remember my first guitar. Mom and I picked it out as a birthday present. It was so beautiful - blonde wood and mother of pearl inlaid at the center. It was as beautiful as I believed I might be able to play some day. A Fender.

I see the a wall of windows and the as morning light that stripe the walls and ceiling, and I see my house

It was grey and white and sat well above the street with steep, concrete steps on both sides. We had flowers and trees and shrubs and weeds. Lots of weeds. It was my job to pluck them.

Our house was old and creaky. The wood floors talked when I walked, a groan, a squeak, noisy boards that made it impossible to sneak in late at night without waking my mother.

playing on the porch

guitar store — buying my first Fender

crowd   me   dreaming of rock star Penny

Cam — teaching my son to play

I play when I work on my writing.

Chapter 2

Understanding Readers and Reading

Why Students Won't Read What We Assign

It's the end of the semester, so I've been interviewing my students all week. I began these interviews years ago in response to my principal's challenge to make listening to students one of our all-school goals. In the face of our increasing dropout rate and low SAT scores, he said we should listen to our students more. It made good sense, but it was a courageous move. Some of my colleagues ignored this goal. They were busy people, too busy. Some risked learning about their own teaching through the eyes of their greatest critics. I decided to ask questions that were nagging at me about teenage reading habits and videotape my students' answers. Seven years later, I am still filming—and still getting the same answers.

On Friday I sat beside Ryan. A determined nonreader, he told me honestly that before he entered my class as a senior, he hadn't read a book since fifth grade. He didn't read the books assigned in English class. He laughed at the suggestion that *anyone* reads those books. He didn't know a single person in College Prep English who actually read *To Kill a Mockingbird* or *The Lord of the Flies*. Those books not only did not entice him to read, they convinced him reading was not for him. Throughout middle and high school whenever his teachers assigned a report on a book of his choice (a common technique to highlight the importance of pleasure reading) he used the same report on *Wringer*, which he had read in fifth grade.

"Did you ever try to read those books assigned to you?" I asked—a new question for me. In the past few years as student after student catalogued his (and her) nonreading habits, I accepted that the books just didn't interest them and they didn't bother reading because pretending to read is so easy. I wondered if students were just lazy or rebellious. Those are adjectives too often used in the staff room to describe today's teenagers, but they do not represent my experience with students, so I pressed farther. My students are anything but lazy readers. They exceed their individual reading goals more often than not, which means they read well beyond two hours outside school week after week. And not just some of my students, almost all of them.

I asked Ryan, "Did you ever try to read the assigned books?" And he and every student I asked said yes. Yes, but only a page or two; yes, but after the first two chapters I figured, why bother? Ryan's answer was revealing. "I tried like the first two chapters, but the next night it would be two or three more, and then two or three more, but it was taking me so long to read and it wasn't getting any better and I was getting farther behind so I just figured why bother? I wasn't understanding any of it anyway." Clearly, he was outmatched by the text.

There is a bidirectional relationship between will and skill, as established in a study by Morgan and Fuchs (2007): "As argued by Spear-Swerling and Sternberg (1994), 'Once children have entered the "swamp" of negative expectations, lowered motivation, and limited practice, it becomes increasingly difficult for them to get back on the road of proficient reading'" (178). Ryan's willingness to read is impacted by his skill level, and his skills, of course, are impacted by his willingness to work on them. These foundations of independent reading are critical to understanding why teenagers have stopped reading in high school.

Frustration undermines the will to read. Ryan did not have the skill to comprehend his reading, so he lost the will to try. Because he won't try, his skills will stagnate. *Ryan isn't trying hard enough*, you might say, but I would add, *and he's in a text that isn't helping him.* As Dick Allington (2009) has said, "In order to read fluently, all readers need texts that they can read with a high degree of accuracy and automaticity. When readers are provided with texts that are too difficult, fluent reading is impossible" (26). If Ryan reads page after page and ends with no understanding, we need to build his capacity as a reader in texts he *can* understand.

Reading Hurdles: Vocabulary, Context, Sentence Length

Accuracy impacts comprehension. Allington suggests that a 98–99 percent accuracy rate is appropriate during independent reading (27)—one or two errors out of a hundred words read. A novel has between two hundred and three hundred words on every page, so even stumbling over five or six words per page, a student could still keep reading without confusion. Once a student is tangled in a text, however, frustration impedes understanding and cripples the will to read. As Allington suggests, "If I were to design a program that would foster dysfluent reading, I would create lessons where readers were given a steady diet of too-difficult texts, texts they cannot read accurately" (34). We need to remember this as we consider increasing complexity in texts. Students need to build stamina for those texts through their independent reading.

I decided to rate the fluency of one page of *Crime and Punishment* (see Figure 2.1) after a frustrated student abandoned it. Renaissance Learning (2012) ranks the reading level of this novel as grade 8.7, but I noticed as I read that the sentences were sometimes so long I felt I was working my way through a labyrinth. Long sentences require a reader to keep a great deal of information in her head and see how clauses relate to the main idea. I kept track of sentence length because I sensed how it would trip up my students. I also underlined words or phrases most of my students wouldn't recognize, knowing it slows readers down and often requires rereading. I then rated the fluency of a page from a book currently popular in my classroom, *The Other Wes Moore* (see Figure 2.2). Both have merits as texts, but *Wes Moore* has a waiting list and *Crime* gathers dust. Jacob had been the first student in years to pull *Crime and Punishment* off the shelf by choice. Which would you more likely read?

Figure 2.1 Crime and Punishment *page*

434 CRIME AND PUNISHMENT
from the day he had moved in with him; yet at the same time he seemed a little <u>apprehensive</u> of him. On arriving in St Petersburg he had put up at his lodgings not merely out of stingy thrift – though that had probably been his main motive – there had *32* been another motive, too. Back in the provinces he had heard of <u>Andrei Semyonovich</u>, his former pupil, as one of the foremost young progressives, who even played a significant role in certain *31* curious and legendary circles. <u>Pyotr Petrovich</u> had been struck *7* by this. For these powerful, <u>omniscient</u> circles with their contempt for everyone and accusations against all and <u>sundry</u> had long inspired <u>Pyotr Petrovich</u> with a peculiar, though wholly *30* vague, sense of terror. It went without saying that, back there in the provinces, he had been unable to form even an approximate *26* conception of *what it was all about*. He had heard, like everyone else, that particularly in St Petersburg there were to be found <u>progressives</u>, <u>nihilists</u>, public accusers, and so on, and so forth, but, like many people, he tended to exaggerate and distort the *49* sense and significance of these labels to the point of the absurd. For several years now he had feared more than anything else being made the victim of a *public accusation*, and this was the principal reason for his constant, exaggerated sense of anxiety, especially when he had dreamt of moving his practice to *44* St Petersburg. In this respect he was, as they say, '<u>affrit</u>', in the way small children sometimes are. Some years earlier, in the provinces, when he had only just been beginning to organize his career, he had encountered two cases involving the merciless public accusation and exposure of rather important persons in local government to whom he had been attached and who had *65* afforded him official protection. One of these cases had ended in a particularly scandalous manner for the man who had been *20* accused, and the other had very nearly ended in outright disaster. This was why <u>Pyotr Petrovich</u> had made it his object to discover, as soon as he arrived in St Petersburg, 'what it was all about' and, if necessary, to get ahead of the game and <u>curry favour</u> *41* with 'our younger generations'. In this matter he had placed his reliance upon <u>Andrei Semyonovich</u> and had, for his visit to <u>Raskolnikov,</u> for example, already learned how to roll off *30* certain phrases parrot-fashion . . .

Figure 2.2 The Other Wes Moore *page*

Introduction
This is the story of two boys living in Baltimore with similar histories and an identical name: Wes Moore. One of us is free and has experi- *19* enced things that he never even knew to dream about as a kid. The *20* other will spend every day until his death behind bars for an armed robbery that left a police officer and father of five dead. The chilling *25* truth is that his story could have been mine. The tragedy is that my *11* story could have been his. Our stories are obviously specific to our *10* two lives, but I hope they will illuminate the <u>crucial inflection points</u> in every life, the sudden moments of decision where our paths diverge and our fates are sealed. It's unsettling to know how little separates *36* each of us from another life altogether. *14*
In late 2000, the *Baltimore Sun* published a short article with the headline "Local Graduate Named Rhodes Scholar." It was about me. *10* As a senior at Johns Hopkins University, I received one of the most *4* prestigious academic awards for students in the world. That fall I was *21* moving to England to attend Oxford University on a full scholarship. *15*
But that story had less of an impact on me than another series of articles in the *Sun*, about an incident that happened just months before, a precisely planned jewelry store robbery gone terribly wrong. *35* The store's security guard—an off-duty police officer named Bruce Prothero—was shot and killed after he pursued the armed men into

I am not making the argument here that one text is better than the other. I am simply saying that one is more likely to be read accurately (independently) than the other. Yes, I can walk Jacob through *Crime and Punishment* page by page and help him understand. In fact, we teachers work hard to summarize and explain a text this challenging. However, our students need to gain facility as independent readers, and without accuracy this just isn't likely. We have to commit to helping students choose texts they can navigate alone, then teach the skills needed to unravel more difficult texts in class, so that their skills increase while they experience the pleasure of reading. When skills and pleasure align, students begin to choose more difficult texts to read independently.

A key factor with this student and this text was Jacob's stamina. When he came to me as a senior he had been fake-reading for years. He found books he liked early in the year and then jumped to *Crime and Punishment* that winter. He worked hard to read it, but finally, after nearly four hundred pages, abandoned it in frustration. Had he been actively working on stamina in the years prior to entering my classroom, I believe he would have finished the book.

This semester I have a junior who has also been a fake reader. Justin has a thin, uninspired history of reading. It's just "not his thing." He found a few books he'd enjoyed in the past and reread them at the start of our time together but often found excuses for not reading regularly. I listened and nudged and when I challenged the whole class to find a "reach" book at the start of fourth quarter, he chose *The Fountainhead*. I asked why. He said it was the fattest book on the shelf in the hardest section: classics. I thought it a wrong choice, but he began it. And kept going. He finished it in seven days. We discussed it for a long while. I have to admit, I kept probing because I wondered if he *had* read it. This seems silly in retrospect. He had no trouble telling me he wasn't a reader, wasn't interested in reading, and he was fine with this identity early in the semester. Why would he lie now? He was eager to talk about the book, and although I never liked it, I remembered enough as I thumbed through it while we talked to engage him. He did most of the talking. He even said, "I know you didn't think I would read it." We teachers are so easy to read.

When I asked Justin what he would read next, he said, "Oh, *The Fountainhead* ought to count for the next month or so." I laughed; he was serious. I needed a good match to entice him to keep reading. I pulled *Townie*, by Andre Dubus III, off the shelf. I've given it to four men I know who are readers and each has confirmed its power. I was absolutely captivated by it. It's a memoir of a young boy in Boston trying to fight his way through life. It's brutal. It's beautiful. Yesterday Justin was a hundred pages in. I said, "Oh, so you're reading it?" He said, "You suggested it, so I am." Both of the books he's chosen this month are huge leaps in complexity and language, and he is increasing his stamina as a reader. However, the language of both is accessible, so I believe his enjoyment is more likely and thus his willingness to keep trying. We can and must give students rich experiences with literature, but we also must pay attention to how texts can discourage them.

It's no secret that many students read thousands of text messages a month and chat online. These forms value brevity. We are all being changed by tweets and increasingly brief emails in which succinct language and efficiency rule. I happened on the 2010 National Book Critics Circle Award winner, *A Visit from the Goon Squad,* by Jennifer Egan, and was intrigued by a chapter narrated by a twelve-year-old who writes in a form she calls a slide journal. It's a chapter of startling creativity with just a few words per page, but the format and the voice lead you in. I felt I was reading a character's private messages—just right for the voice of a teenager in a book that has a different narrator for each chapter.

Good writing exists in any form, of course, and those forms they are a-changin', as Bob Dylan would say. What I seek is access to any text form. When a student won't read, I look at the vocabulary, the context of the book, and the sentence length to see whether the text is a mismatch for the student's current skills. If I'm going to improve reading, students must practice reading skills in a text better matched to their ability and then continue to encounter more challenging texts as they increase volume and stamina.

We teach students first, then curriculum. It is not going to be easy to lead all our students to literature. But we can't give up, either.

How Many Nonreaders Are Out There?

This is how most people live:
sleeping on the bank of a fresh-water stream, lips dry with thirst.

—Rumi

Now that I'm asking the question, I've discovered that most teachers know many students aren't reading. I've asked groups of teachers in nearly every state and almost all the Canadian provinces. I get similar answers. Teachers tell me they think about 20 percent or fewer of their students actually read the literature assigned. Some books reach more students, but over the course of the year, how many of your students read regularly?

Teachers still teach books they know most kids won't read; they do it because they feel pressured by their curriculum. They pace the reading so it's not overwhelming for those who struggle, but they know they are selling the best readers short by moving so slowly. These are troubling adaptations in classrooms of mixed abilities in a high-pressure, never-enough-time age. Yet if you teach English in middle or high school, you've probably faced this dilemma. What to do?

First of all, we have to quit pretending that nonreading is somehow not our responsibility. As Kelly Gallagher says in *Readicide* (2009), "Never lose sight that our highest priority is to raise students who become lifelong readers. What our students read in school is important; what they read the rest of their lives is more important" (117). We are expected to create lifelong readers. I believe it is our most important goal. But when my beliefs do not align with my practices, I lose the energy to teach.

Bear with me for one last example of the complexity of this problem. Zach is in my twelfth-grade class and all my efforts to engage him with books are failing. He tells me he's never seen a movie in his mind when he reads. And this kid loves movies. He tells me that if he could see what he's reading, he'd read. He never has. Reading to him is a dull, monotonous voice—just words on the page. It is hard for him to listen well—or care. He stopped trying to read early in elementary school. He's had lots of interventions, but he never—ever—found a book he wanted to read. I can't believe anyone thinks *Julius Caesar* is the next best choice for him.

What's engaged reading for him? *National Geographic*. He likes the combination of pictures and text. And he chooses which articles to read and which to skip. Over the last month he's read seven pages in a novel he's chosen to read in my class. He's read almost all of several *National Geographic* magazines.

I believe books matter. I believe it is important to help Zach find a book that will lead him to sustained engagement with an idea or story over hundreds of pages, deepening his thinking. This prepares him for the sustained thinking in texts he'll encounter as an adult. But I bide my time. I let him find pleasure in reading *something* before I push for a longer text. That's the art of this work. Teaching reading will never be a script of simple steps at the end of which all readers become proficient. Teaching is far more complex than any publisher or program can imagine. But teaching is the only way to improve readers.

Everything I Needed to Know I Learned on My Guitar

Paul broke free from our father's instruction into a rhythm all his own.

—*Norman Maclean,* **A River Runs Through It**

I crave distractions when I'm struggling to revise. Last week I stopped trying to make a draft work and reached behind me for my son's guitar. My Fender, my first guitar, still has a beautiful sound, but the one that sits in my office now is Cam's. It is smaller, all black, and it fits my body better. I can change chords with ease. The memory of rhythm comes back the moment it is cradled in my arms. I'm back on the porch of our house on Belmont Street. The trees move in the wind. The sky is blue, fading to dusk. I swagger to the edge of the porch like I'm on stage—imagine Joan Jett in black leather. I call to the squirrels and raccoons that roam the border of our yard, "Thank you for being here tonight." I play my first chords to the sky and sink into sound. The tension of being fifteen eases. I play for hours.

Even today I feel the effortlessness I experienced as a teenager during the thousands of hours I spent listening, tuning, and practicing on the back porch. I open the music for "I'd Rather Be with You," by Joshua Radin, a current favorite, and imagine playing alongside my son. I love the way strings lead that song.

In the years when I played my guitar every day I relaxed into rhythm. I learned to move before the stroke, to feel where the guitar players I listened to were headed. I studied classical guitar in college, and when I made the leap to reading music, I played with an attention to each note, a focus that led me to hear all music differently. I didn't know what I didn't know before then.

It's a good thing I have a high tolerance for approximation, though, because today my fingertips have lost their calluses, I stumble through chords that used to be simple, and I tire easily. The guitar has to be tuned almost every time I play because it sits too long unused and I have no tolerance for discord. But I've missed playing. What brought me back? It was the memory of beauty. I once could play, and I loved it.

Practice, of course, is most important. Anything we learn to do well follows the arc from stumbling to competence to confidence to stretching toward what feels impossible. You've heard of Malcolm Gladwell's 10,000 hours rule: the key to success in any field has little to do with talent, it's simply practice, 10,000 hours of it—twenty hours a week for ten years (Grossman 2008).

Volume matters.

I learned with my guitar that even if you leave a skill you once knew well, years later you retain the memory of rhythm thrumming somewhere inside you. I can tune to it and find my way. When my approximations start getting closer, I enjoy playing more. I start reaching for the guitar every afternoon, even for just ten minutes a day. I play to what I can't do yet but know will come.

What I want, though, is to reach behind my desk and just play like I used to. I want to blast along with Mumford & Sons' "Winter Winds" without the months it would take for me to approach even a tolerable imitation. And I know where that comes from: I play air guitar in my car much too often. Air guitar makes me feel I know how to play: pretend competence. The real thing is infinitely harder, of course—and infinitely more satisfying.

Too many people in power think reading is the sum of its parts, so we've got all these kids playing air guitar, if you will, with short passages and questions and multiple-choice answers. These abbreviated bits of reading are not the real thing.

Passages lack wholeness and feel like work without purpose. When we then give students books, thinking they can transfer their practice or that they'll even want to, we're surprised they don't have the interest or the stamina for it.

No one cares whether I can play a G chord. They want to hear a song. When I practiced chords the summer I first picked up a guitar, I always practiced them in songs. No kid should be mindlessly, endlessly practicing parts. They need to be reading books: books that move them, books that they follow and learn the rhythm of. And they need time to reread, because they'll know more when they do. Rereading is like playing the same song over and over, not only because I crave its familiarity but because I see and hear more the more carefully I listen. And the better I get at anticipating where the song is going, the more I can begin to put the parts together that help me know the whole of it.

Rhythm is about listening and "feel" and then finally creation. When you master imitation, you're ready to move your work beyond what you hear in others' to what you hear in your own. That's all of it, I think. That's writing and reading and thinking with words, isn't it? When you read well, you hear how the parts work together. Once you can do that, you can create writing from parts to a whole you couldn't imagine before.

My wish is for students to break free from instruction in parts to the beauty of literature found in a rhythm of their own, one that feels what I cannot, one that finds connections and discovers authors and works I've never heard of. I want students who tune the words they find to who they are. This will come only with practicing the whole of reading, writing, and listening to words.

The Volume of Reading in English Class

Teenagers must read more; I believe all English teachers would agree. The best fiction and literary nonfiction electrifies. Students must know the potency of great writing, and there is so much of it. I am relocated from my small New Hampshire town to a pickup truck racing across Oklahoma as dust blackens the horizon in Timothy Egan's *The Worst Hard Time: The Untold Story of Those Who Survived the Great American Dust Bowl*. There are journal entries here, I tell my students, that take you inside the life, the fear, and the courage of that time. I can agonize alongside a young girl anticipating an arranged marriage in *The Bookseller of Kabul*, trying to understand a culture so unlike my own. Literature reshapes my ordinary life into high adventure. I climb Mt. Everest in a blizzard in Jon Krakauer's *Into Thin Air*. I panic in the uncertainty of a tsunami in Jhumpa Lahiri's *Unaccustomed Earth* and suddenly have to know more about all the lives swept away in 2004. One moment in one book leads me to weeks of reading newspaper articles, following a trail of stories. I look at a library and see gifts. There are simply so many astonishing stories to share. Why aren't our students reading them?

Here's one reason: English class has been dominated for decades by a few titles carefully parceled out chapter by chapter, year by year. We hold the keys to a library of increasing size and depth, but we steer kids to a small collection of titles and say, "These are the best, and we're going to study them thoroughly. We'll spend weeks on each one because in high school we study literature, we don't read and enjoy books. If you're interested in those other books, you can read those on your own time." Too many students are left with an abridged view of an expansive field, as if four or six or ten novels are enough reading for anyone in a school year, let alone developing readers we are trying to prepare for the increasing literacy demands of a modern world.

Students need guidance to choose well and develop sustained independent engagement. Many teachers don't know the great literature that is written just for teenagers, so they suggest more classics, which narrows the likelihood of additional reading to the students who already read. Our disinterested and struggling readers don't know how to choose books that match their passions and abilities, and without attention, they drift along without reading, or when pressed, they choose what's popular, not what's truly terrific writing. Popular fiction can entertain, but it rarely leaves students stunned by insight or transfixed by the resiliency of humanity. Literature is more than action and characters, and my mission is for every student to own this distinction.

What I am proposing in this book runs parallel to the accepted structure of English class. The study of literature is half the job; leading students to satisfying and challenging reading lives is the other, and we haven't paid enough attention to it. Studying literature often requires students to examine books they are unprepared to read, fails to give students enough practice in sustained reading, and often fails to develop a love of books. Although we may pass on a bit of cultural knowledge, reading classics rarely helps most students develop the commitment, stamina, and pleasure in reading that will last. We need a system for matching kids to books they'll love and monitoring their use of strategies that deepen comprehension, and we need teachers who will nudge them to increase the complexity of their reading over time.

It feels radical to suggest we look at individual students instead of groups in a time when the Common Core Initiative is driving thinking in education, but a reading appetite is quirky, singular, and essential. At the core of what I know about students, teaching, and learning is passionate engagement. Passions are peculiar, but passions drive readers to devour books.

Developing Stamina for College and Beyond

This book began by chance. I ran into a former middle school student of mine while getting coffee one morning on my way to school. I said, "Hey—what are you doing home? Didn't you go to UNH last year?"

He smirked. "Yeah, I didn't do that well. It was a lot of work, Mrs. Kittle. A lot of reading." I nodded. "Yeah, well, after I left your class I never read much in high school." Matt's admission stayed with me all that day. I kept thinking that his one year of college (and the nearly $20K in debt that came with it) wasn't going to help him meet any of his aspirations. It was almost worse than never going at all. This bright, capable young man should have succeeded. What had happened?

I emailed four professor friends that night and asked a simple question: *How much does a freshman in college need to read to keep up?* I also asked, *Is there any particular book that you hope all high school students will read before they come to college?*

The long responses (especially from Tom Newkirk at the University of New Hampshire and my brother-in-law Peter Kittle from Chico State University) sent me on a journey. I remember Tom's distinctly. He said he didn't care whether all students read any particular book, only that they read a lot so they would have a variety of experiences to draw on and the ability to handle the volume of reading expected in college. Peter said if students were readers, they were prepared. I started emailing professors I'd never heard of on campuses all over the United States and Canada. Many never responded, but those who did stressed volume. I got a wide range of answers, but 200–600 pages a week was common. I knew most of my students were not prepared for this.

Figure 2.3 *Portrait of a Failing System*

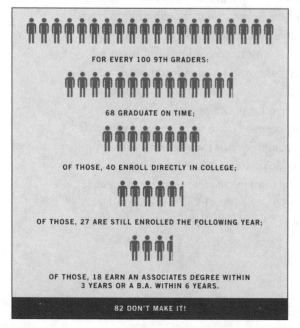

FOR EVERY 100 9TH GRADERS:

68 GRADUATE ON TIME;

OF THOSE, 40 ENROLL DIRECTLY IN COLLEGE;

OF THOSE, 27 ARE STILL ENROLLED THE FOLLOWING YEAR;

OF THOSE, 18 EARN AN ASSOCIATES DEGREE WITHIN
3 YEARS OR A B.A. WITHIN 6 YEARS.

82 DON'T MAKE IT!

I continue to ask former students how much reading they are doing in college. Henny, currently enrolled at Harvard, said he is assigned 400 pages a week for one class. My daughter, now entering her senior year at Providence College, has had 600 pages a week assigned each week for the last three years. I consistently hear 100–600 pages a week from current college students.

The National Center on Education and the Economy's *Tough Choices or Tough Times* (2007) includes the graph in Figure 2.3. I wonder about the large number of students who do not return to college sophomore year. Economics is a factor, to be sure, but could it also be about reading?

In a book titled *Crossing the Finish Line*, the authors, William Bowen, president of Princeton for eighteen years, and Michael McPherson, former Macalaster College president, studied 200,000 students at 68 colleges. They found that only 33 percent of the freshmen who enter the University of Massachusetts, Boston, graduate within six years. Less than 41 percent graduate from the University of Montana, and 44 percent from the University of New Mexico. It seems obvious to me. If students like Matt enter college as practiced nonreaders, they will likely become part of the large number of students who will not finish. Something has to change in high school to prepare kids better.

It can be hard to discuss this idea with colleagues. I find teachers stridently defend one focus for our teaching or the other in polarizing discussions. Curriculum is presented as either "a rigorous study of the classics" or "free reading of what's easy." There seems little room for complexity in thinking about the balance and about volume. I am suggesting that teaching English can't be one or the other; it has to be both.

Finding Lessons for Life

Most of the literature we study in high school was written by adults for adults, and they're good books—some are great books—but they're just not interesting to almost all teenagers. The casualty of disinterest is not reading. You know it. I know it. Adolescents will use a shortcut like SparkNotes to fake it through class when they don't value the work. Some teachers devise difficult or tricky quizzes ("I only quiz them on the details not listed on SparkNotes," one teacher boasted) to catch the nonreaders and punish them. These quizzes often breed resentment, even from compliant readers. "I did the reading," one tenth-grade honors student shouted at me in the hall, "but he asked these four stupid questions I didn't remember and I got a 50 on the quiz! It's not right!" Forest's teacher assured him there would be lots of quizzes and the lowest grade would be dropped, but for Forest this wasn't worry, it was fury. "Why is school this game?" he challenged me one afternoon. Forest had been a greedy reader in my ninth-grade class, finishing thirty-eight books, but now his rich and varied reading life had been reduced to six books—six!—in sophomore year. Four of those books were "mediocre at best," he said. "Everything is so slow"—I remember the way he glanced up at the clock as he tossed a lacrosse stick back and forth—"the hands stop in English class." His teacher did not expect him to read more than that, so he read little. Eventually he used SparkNotes to pass the quizzes and skipped the reading altogether.

We need students who evaluate online claims and become critical thinkers of an ever expanding array of texts. We need to measure comprehension and give students tools to understand difficult texts, but they also need sustained engagement with stories through hundreds of pages of text. Why story? Because, as Dennis Dutton details in *The Art Instinct*, "imagination allows the weighing of indirect evidence, making chains of inference for what might have been or what might come to be. It allows for intellectual simulation and forecasting, the working out of solutions to problems without high-cost experimentation in actual practice" (2009, 105). Students must read literature that names what they themselves struggle to understand. This semester Kyle is reading about the cataclysmic progression of drug abuse and Jonah is reading his third novel about sexual identity. They are finding answers in young adult literature to their own questions. I can't help but remember my own impulsivity as a high school freshman. Had I been reading a book like *She's Got Next* I might have stayed with basketball instead of swapping it for cheerleading. When we enter the sound and images of a story—led by a writer's vision and voice—we live within a blend of our own experiences and those in the book. The novels in my freshman English class were all about adults with adult problems, not kids like me, so I couldn't experiment with solutions through fiction.

Life lessons live in fiction. Reading a book takes us inside a time, a place, or an idea. Show me the grime on the streets of London and let me watch as skeletal children dash after the coal cart in rags in Charles Dickens' *The Tale of Two Cities*. As Dickens reaches deeper into the images, feelings, and sounds of that time, he makes room for ideas: hunger, children, want, excess, waste. When I walk for a few hours beside such brutality, how can I escape being changed by it? I look up from Dickens' words to my living room and see differently—want to live differently perhaps.

This is what books can do, but only if the reader is deeply engaged with the text. It is through the complexity of the story that we can be changed, as Dutton (2009) says, because it provides "a useful set of templates and examples to guide and inspire human action" (111). What we deeply desire for students to know—that art imitates life—their life—can be lost to them. They will solve their life problems through talk, through high-risk experimentation, perhaps, but not through books.

Imagine how this plays out into decisions in our democratic society. Why do so many embrace abbreviated news coverage instead of the in-depth world news in *The New York Times*? Why listen to the thirty-second sound-bite instead of reading the intricacies of a local school budget? We want to understand the choices before us, but have we replaced reading with television to fulfill this instinct? I confess I've never watched more than a few minutes of one of the many *Real Housewives* shows, but surely they represent the fantasy of having limitless funds for beautiful clothes and age-defying cosmetic surgeries. Viewers can watch and judge, imagining their own better choices perhaps, but I would prefer they read *Anna Karenina* when faced with the seduction of a man who seems to offer what is missing in a marriage. Not only because they can live out the cost of following selfish desire without actually experiencing it and damaging so many innocents, but because of Levin and Kitty, the other story arc in this complex novel, who open up possibility for a life of faith and commitment. And the novel transcends both stories to teach a slice of Russian experience and history seen through the mind of an author in love with words and beautifully constructed sentences. You might laugh at the idea that the average *Real Housewives* viewer might choose Tolstoy, but this is my point. Why are we creating only a very few readers in high school who might choose Tolstoy? I want more of them. Voluminous, voracious readers are our only hope.

I believe Brycen, an eighth grader who has read *War*, *The Good Soldiers*, *Sniper*, *Lost in Kandahar*, and *Task Force Black* this year, could make a more informed decision about the American occupation of Iraq now than most adults who have the power to do so. If he had not been allowed to read those books, had been given only the texts that illustrate the complexity band for grades 6–8 in the Common Core State Standards (a list of literary and informational texts published between 1869 and 1976), he would have missed the blend of informational texts and literature that has become a passion for him. He would also have missed his life as a reader that he now sees evolving with endless possibilities.

Every student needs to know the power of a reading life. Dickens simply won't matter to most twenty-first-century teenagers unless they have developed a love of books first—a trust that even the most difficult ones can be worthwhile. We can and must develop that trust every year in school.

The amount of reading students do matters. To be engaged with the deep reading of literature, you first have to be comfortable with words, lots of them over hundreds of pages. Our students need to read dozens and dozens of books a year. Not all these books will be classic literature, but some will be. I know they'll read more literature in high school with this approach than if we stick to the few books a year we have in place now. As my friend Timothy Pruzinski, an International Baccalaureate (IB) teacher at the International School Bangkok and IB teacher trainer told me, "At the most, in higher-level literature, the IB requires students to read 13 texts over two years. My breakdown is four plays, two novels, two anthologies of short stories, one graphic novel, one poet and one survey of poetry, one book of creative nonfiction, as well as one survey of essays. Other teachers will have a different assortment of texts, but the reality is that students will read on average 6.5 texts a year." Tim realizes this is simply not enough reading and has added a focus on building the reading lives of his students, but he is rare. We all must aim higher. Let's start with at least twenty-five books a year, grades 6–12, so that all students reach for a goal of 175–200 books in adolescence. Many will read many more. Some of those books will be read slowly over time with a teacher, but others will be read at the student's own rate for interest and joy. This is possible.

Developing reading stamina by cultivating an individual reading habit requires relationships with students and systems that support, encourage, and challenge readers; it also requires will. The teachers I admire commit themselves to every student every year. That is the necessary foundation for this work: the will to lead students from popular fiction to increasingly complex texts, fiction or nonfiction. I believe no one wants to live on candy all the time, even teenagers. I've seen a hunger develop in so many students who seemed content with popular romances when they entered my classroom. When they finally made the leap to choosing literature, they could feel the difference for themselves. They wanted more. They read more. They read far more than we expect of them now.

The one element of high school English you won't find developed in this book is how to study one novel as a whole class. It isn't that I don't value this practice. I do. Discussions that lead students to wrestle with meaning and think differently are powerful in the hands of a vibrant, thoughtful teacher and in the hands of students who have read and thought about their reading, grappling with meaning as a teacher stands aside to listen. There are many good books in the world already about this practice of studying literature, and I have nothing to add. I suggest *Notice and Note*, by Kylene Beers and Robert Probst, or *Doing Literary Criticism*, by Tim Gillespie, or *What's the Big Idea?*, by Jim Burke. *Book Love* focuses on managing, sustaining, and building an independent reading life in middle and high school.

Lead from your reading life. I keep a current reading list in my writing notebook, just as I expect my students to.

November cont.

ⓓ 128. Great House Nicole Krausse
129. Academically Adrift Arum, Richard & Josipa Roksa
130. The Geography of Bliss Eric Weiner
131. The Wild Things Dave Eggers
132. Okay for Now Gary Schmidt
ⓓ 133. The Art of Slow Reading Tom Newkirk
134. Wonderstruck Brian Selznick

December 2011

135. Black and White Paul Voloponi
136. Please Ignore Vera Dietz A.S. King
137. delirium Lauren Oliver
138. Write Like This Kelly Gallagher
139. Following Atticus Tom Ryan
140. Encyclopedia of an Ordinary Life Amy Rosenthal
141. How to Save a Life Sarah Zarr
142. Falling for Hamlet Michelle Ray
143. Letters from a Dead Girl Jo Knowles
144. 10 Things Every Writer Needs to Know Jeff Anderson
    (142 total in 2011)

January 2012

1. Salvage the Bones Jesmyn Ward
② How We Are Hungry Dave Eggers
③ Anna Karenina Leo Tolstoy
4. State of Wonder Ann Patchett
5. The Sense of an Ending Julian Barnes
6. The Fault in Our Stars John Greene
7. The Power of Reading Stephen Krashen
8. Glaciers Alexis M. Smith
9. Divergent Veronica Roth
10. Hound Dog True Linda Urban

February 2012

11. Black Like Me John Howard Griffin
12. What Teaching Really Means various authors
13. The Five Dysfunctions of a Team Patrick Lencioni
14. Is Everybody Having Fun without Me? Mindy Kaling

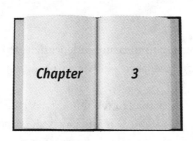

Chapter 3

Building Stamina and Fluency

Setting Realistic and Challenging Weekly Goals

During the first week of class I ask students to find a book they would like to read and to read silently, at a comfortable pace, for ten minutes. I emphasize the importance of reading at a pace where the text is making sense—slow reading to enter the story, not skimming like they do online. If rereading increases understanding, do it. The goal is understanding, not speed. I also seek confidence in readers and the idea that reading can be enjoyable—twin goals that run throughout my teaching. At the end of ten minutes each student records the number of pages read in that time. I make sure my students understand that this reading rate is for the current book they're reading and really says nothing about them as a reader. What I'm trying to establish is a measure to make the homework reading I'm going to assign fair to all.

Students read at vastly different rates, even if assigned to a leveled English class. Richard Allington (2001) analyzed the words per minute for *Hatchet*, by Gary Paulsen, and found that it would take an average fifth grader eight hours to read it, so a student reading at half that speed would need sixteen hours (36–37). This means the typical English class assignment of two chapters a night might take Heather twenty minutes and Andre three hours. I am not exaggerating this gap, since I have measured it with my seniors. I tell my students their homework is to read at a comfortable pace for two hours or more each week outside class. In order for that to be a fair assignment, I explain, we need to determine an individual reading rate. It can also help us understand how their pace changes over the course of a quarter, a semester, and a school year with regular reading.

I recognize that this is not a scientific measure. I am not a fluency expert. I'm a classroom teacher trying to devise a way to challenge all my readers to read more each week. I don't want to improve the stamina of just my lowest-skilled readers but to challenge my strongest readers to read more widely and deeply than they have in the past. I need a way to measure independent reading that empowers and encourages students to improve their skills at a pace that honors the efforts of all the readers in the room.

Each student records pages read in ten minutes. A student who reads nine pages multiplies nine by six to calculate how many pages she can comfortably read in that book in one hour. Doubling it results in her expected-pages-per-week goal ($9 \times 6 = 54 \times 2 = 108$ pages per week). I also explain that increasing stamina means they may only read for ten minutes at a time at first but should gradually increase to an hour or more in one sitting. This alone is a challenge, and students must learn strategies for building stamina. As a senior, Colton, wrote on his final exam, "I have never been a reader, so when I started to have trouble while reading a book, I would take like a five-minute break just to get my mind off it so it was fresh to come back and try to tackle it again. I learned that reading isn't as bad as I made it out to be in the past. In the past I made myself try and drag through other books, but then I just gave up." When students measure stamina through pages read each week, it is easier for them to see growth and also to keep track of the reading they need to do for homework.

Students have an intuitive sense that reading rate varies based on the difficulty of the text, so we discuss how changing books puts different demands on them as readers and may require calculating a new reading rate. Since we read for at least ten minutes in class each day, a new rate is easily determined. In order to receive full credit for homework, each student needs to meet or exceed his or her reading goal each week. Students record their rates in their writing notebooks, which I collect so I can record individual rates in my own records. Over the year I record a student's reading rate at least once a month, but numbers alone do not tell the story. Many students see a decline in reading rate because they begin to choose more difficult books as they become more confident readers. All students begin to work toward the college expectation of at least two hundred pages a week, no matter how many hours it takes them. I think the combination of a long-term goal and monitoring progress on a weekly goal is important. Students need both.

In my class this fall the range of reading rates was wide. Richard could read 60 pages in two hours, Melinda read 92, and Ciera read 312. Lissa read 32, but considering that was more than she remembered reading since elementary school, I considered it quite an achievement when she beat that goal every one of our first five weeks of school. Students record the title of the book they are reading and the page they are on every day in class, adding up the total pages read each week (see Figure 3.1). Students are expected to find the time to read during the week, but if sports or other responsibilities intrude, they can catch up on the weekend. What I don't accept is the excuse that they can't find the time at all. They can. They do. We calculate total pages for the week each Monday, and the majority of my students beat their reading goal almost every week all year.

Figure 3.1 *Weekly reading recording sheet*

December 15

808
249
260 "Scribble. That's what I tell all the writers I meet. Don't sit down to write a book, just start to scribble."
499 — Frank McCourt, author of *Angela's Ashes*

Student Name	Book title.........	Mon.	Tues.	Wed.	Thurs.	Fri.	Total pages
	Deadline,	227	227	246	271	271	85
	Keeping the moon	1	52	101	90	112 / 111	202
	Paper towns	12	90	196	305	25	
	The Lost Five Scur...	156	167	185	202	215 / 59	
	The Killing hour	1	12	29	55	78 / 70	265
	The Space Between	162	246	43	167	241	250
	The OATH	17	31	65			87
	1984		31	50	78	130	
	Twilight	34	80		236	306	537
	True Believer	110	130	157	172		
	True Believer	160	193	219	245	264 / 104	111
	Water for Elephants	1	20	107	82	299	259
	The Double Bind	4	9	37	53	89	259
	In Cold Blood	6	17	24	36	49	109
	Twilight	280	305	318	335	354	160
	Forever changes/feelings	39	75	118	1	22	287
	So long and thanks for all the	657	616		788	813	228
	Frozen Fire	1	49	119	528	0-45	205
	Someone Like You	127	180	219	10	55	133
	2 the next street		25	42	64	81	110
	Honey Baby Sweetheart			20		29 / 40	147
	An abundance of katherines	15	45	77	90	150 / 135	251
	The Kite Runner	83	96	109	117	124	83
	White Oleander	151	168	192	204		98
	Into the Wild	23	37	42	72	81	151

Goals are important. When investigating what teachers can do to boost motivation, Quirk and Schwanenflugel (2004) found: "Researchers advise practitioners to help children self-set goals that are challenging but reachable. A teacher might spend a few minutes each week helping a child monitor his or her progress in meeting these goals. Accomplishing these goals may bolster the child's belief that, with effort, he or she can become a better reader." Weekly goals help me convince my students that they can improve with practice, but the goals don't turn them into readers. The wonder, the magic, and the heart-stopping joy of books is the only consistently effective tool for that.

Keeping Track of What Twenty-Five Students Are Doing in Twenty-Five Books

The recording sheet in Figure 3.1, which makes its way around the room during our daily silent reading, lets me see at a glance which students are reading at night and which are not. Since the reading rates are not on the sheet, there is nothing to hide. Contrary to what some believe, students are honest. Will students cheat? Yes. How many? Remarkably few. My students know I value honesty and want to help them.

They also know they can catch up on the weekend, so they do tell me what they've read each night. Every day when we read in class I can see their engagement. When it is clear a student is bored with the book, I stop by for a conference. I confer with several students about their reading every day, so this isn't unusual. Students take note of what others are reading, but most fill in their page number and pass our recording sheet on quickly in order to get back to their book. I know teachers who keep track themselves via roll call, and on some days I carry the clipboard with me and record the page for each student in the room. It is a nice way to check in with everyone, but it can't take the place of a reading conference. The truth is, when we trust students and help them find books, they rise to our expectations in remarkable ways.

Goals for a Semester or a Year

This spring I tried an experiment with a semester-long elective English class of grade 10–12 mixed-ability students. Five weeks into the semester we used ten minutes of silent reading to calculate the pages per week they could read comfortably. I then asked them to take the pages per week and multiply it by 18 weeks in a semester. We then divided the total pages by 200—since two hundred pages is a reasonable length for a book. Students did the math and arrived at their goal for number of books to read that semester.

I shared reading lists from students I had the year before (see Figures 3.2 and 3.3).

I showed them interviews with both girls who confessed to being nonreaders before coming to my class. I challenged my students to consider what they could accomplish in just one semester. You might think I'm crazy. Many of the kids did.

We discovered that all the students could realistically read between ten and thirty books during the semester. I explained that this represented two hours of reading outside of school each week, that's all. As they got to work on writing that day, I went to each student individually and wrote down the number of books they had calculated and said, "What do you think? Can you do it?" Every student in the class except two said yes. Both girls who said no had calculated more than fifteen books and hadn't read that many books since picture books in elementary school. I assured them they could if they found the right books. This big goal-setting moment is going to happen in each of my classes every September. I will nurture the commitment; I will keep track of progress; I will dare them not to become readers.

To Grade or Not to Grade?

Grades, stickers, star charts, and prizes are all unnecessary rewards in the process of creating readers. As Alfie Kohn (1993) says, we punish students with rewards. Books matter; the rest just gets in the way. I must pay attention to whether or not

Figure 3.2 *Meaghan's reading ladder*

BOOK LIST RANKED MOST DIFFICULT (1) TO EASIEST (23)

1. *Lolita*, Vladimir Nabokov
2. *Columbine*, Dave Cullen
3. *Incendiary*, Chris Cleave
4. *They Poured Fire on Us from the Sky*, Benson Deng, Alephonsion Den, Benjamin Ajak
5. *The Color Purple*, Alice Walker
6. *Lost in the Meritocracy*, Walter Kirn
7. *The Freedom Writers Diary*, Erin Gruwell
8. *Scratch Beginnings*, Chris Crutcher
9. *One Amazing Thing*, Chitra Banerjee Divakaruni
10. *The Other Wes Moore*, Wes Moore
11. *The Curious Incident of the Dog in the Nighttime*, Mark Haddon
12. *Little Bee*, Chris Cleave
13. *After the Wreck*, Joyce Carol Oates
14. *Because I Am Furniture*
15. *Memoirs of a Teenage Amnesiac*, Gabrielle Zevin
16. *Winter Girls*, Laurie Halse Anderson
17. *Twisted*, Laurie Halse Anderson
18. *If I Stay*, Gayle Forman
19. *People Are Unappealing*, Sarah Barron
20. *Inexcusable*
21. *Shooting Kabul*
22. *A Bend in the Road*, Nicholas Sparks
23. *Rules*, Cynthia Lord

Total pages read quarter 4: 2715/9=302

Q1=192, Q2=169, Q3=70, Q4=302

My reading rate increased significantly from quarter 1 to quarter 4. Quarter 3 was so low because I was reading *Lolita* pretty much the whole quarter and quarter 2 I was doing college applications, but I am very surprised by how much it increased over all. It is obvious that the amount I read changes depending on what the book is.

kids are reading. I must observe and talk with kids every day. I keep track of page numbers as a way to manage the large number of students in my classes. However, the weekly goal in reading has to be about more than a grade or a calculation or we'll never create readers.

I consider all grading a necessary evil. It is healthier to assess progress through deep discussions about books and ideas, but changing assessment measures in this country is a battle for someone else to fight. My interest is in improving literacy within the confines of my current school system, and I live in the world of points and grade, so I've compromised.

Figure 3.3 *Taylor's reading ladder*

TAYLOR'S READING LADDER, QUARTER 4

Order by Difficulty (1=most difficult)

1. *Lolita* by Vladimir Nabokov, 317 pp.
2. *Columbine* by Dave Cullen, 370 pp.
3. *The White Tiger* by Aravind Adiga, 304 pp.
4. *Say You're One of Them* by Uwem Akpan, abandoned at page 75.
5. *Slumdog Millionaire* by Vikas Swarup, 336 pp.
6. *The Freedom Writers' Diary* by various writers, 285 pp.
7. *Hunger Games* by Suzanne Collins, 384 pp.
8. *Water for Elephants* by Sara Gruen, 335 pp.
9. *The Perks of Being a Wallflower* by Stephen Chbosky, 213 pp.
10. *Because I Am Furniture* by Thalia Chaltas, 352 pp.
11. *Hate List* by Jennifer Brown, 405 pp.
12. *Miles from Nowhere* by Nami Mun, 286 pp.
13. *Go Ask Alice* by Anonymous, 193 pp.
14. *Shooting Kabul* by N. H. Senzai, 253 pp.
15. *I Am Messenger* by Markus Suzak, abandoned at page 105.
16. *Deadlines* by Chris Crutcher, 316 pp.
17. *If I Stay* by Gayle Forman, 201 pp.
18. *Brutal* by Mark Harmon, 227 pp.
19. *Wintergirls* by Laurie Halse Sanderson, 278 pp.
20. *Twisted* by Laurie Halse Sanderson, 272 pp.
21. *Memoirs of a Teenage Amnesiac* by Gabrielle Zevin, 271 pp.
22. *The Disreputable History of Frankie Landau-Bates* by E. Lockhart, 342 pp.
23. *The Secret Story of Sonia Rodriguez* by Alan Lawrence Sitomer, 311 pp.
24. *I Hope They Serve Beer in Hell* by Tucker Max, 326 pp.

Total pages read during Q4: 1318/9 = 146.4 pages per week

Comparison: First quarter my average reading rate was around 180 pages per week and my second quarter rate was slightly larger. I was reading easier and lighter books; I think that played a huge role in my rates. Third quarter my reading rate went down to 124 pages per week. Even though it was lower, I was more satisfied with my book choices. Fourth quarter I read 146 pages per week. My reading rate went up this quarter because I had more time to read and I think my books were easier. Honestly, I think I became lazier in the fourth quarter.

I give students a weekly grade for homework reading, and these grades are 10 percent of their course grade. I tell them that reading for two hours a week outside class is essential for their stamina as readers. It is a reasonable expectation for teenagers. It should be pleasurable—I emphasize that—but it has to happen. If they meet their reading goal for the week, they get full credit. If they fall short, they get partial credit. I don't share a formula for determining partial credit; that's my decision, which I negotiate with individual students. However, a student who reads anything at all never gets less than 50 percent—I believe in "The Case Against the Zero" (Reeves 2004). My students quickly lose interest in the grade as they find books they want to read.

Increasing Complexity over Time

What do we want from the books students read in class? We want joy, yes, but we also must expect an increased complexity of texts over time. We want our students to be climbers. We want progress in their ability to read. It isn't enough to encourage kids to read outside class and expect somehow that it will happen. But it is also not enough to have kids read one easy junk title after another. Kids can get stuck—as can adults—on a genre or an author. It is true that being stuck can have its benefits I read my way through all of Wallace Stegner's books one summer, then all of Ian McEwan's the next, just as I had read all of the Brontës, then Edith Wharton, and yes, tried but failed to read all of Henry James. I learned more about each writer as I looked at early and late books and began to see patterns emerge in the composition of a novel. Getting stuck can be powerful. Jake read all of Orwell while in my class as a senior, but I see other teenagers get stuck and I think, I want more for you.

Parker—graduating third in her class and heading off to Tulane in the fall on a full scholarship—transferred into my class halfway through her senior year. She had spent her first semester reading pop fiction, and this became the subject of our first January reading conference. "Why are you continuing to read books by this author?" I asked, with genuine curiosity. New to my class, she probably thought she was in trouble. She mumbled a vague, "Yeah, I should read harder books," and ducked behind her bangs.

"My intent is not to make you feel badly about your reading choices, Parker. I read easy, light romances and other escape books." I pointed to my current reading list in my notebook. We both snickered at *Manny*, by Holly Peterson. I continued, "But I wonder why your list lacks variety. I get tired of books that don't challenge me. I crave something that will surprise me—surprise me with the skill of the writer—the knowledge of a place I'll probably never visit—the deep exploration of questions about life that I didn't even know I was asking. Do you ever feel tired of the same old thing in these books?" She nodded. I got to the heart of why I thought she was stuck. "What's on your to-read-next list?" I asked and turned her notebook to the last page.

She didn't have one.

My colleague, Parker's teacher first semester, is a dynamic teacher who has begun integrating book talks into her teaching. But she has yet to develop a systematic approach to two things that really matter if we want to move kids from where they are to where we want them to be: the to-read-next list, so each reader has a plan; and reading conferences that put the teacher one-on-one with a student, asking where she is in her independent reading and what she plans to read next.

Of course, the other students in the room also matter. Parker sits at a table with two other girls. As they recommend books they've read, she will likely be infected by their enthusiasm. If she follows their lead, she'll see the difference for herself as she makes the leap to deep engagement with literature, biography, and nonfiction. This is why I have students create reading progress reflections each quarter and update their goals so that I can continually nudge each one to reach for more (see p. 124 and Figures 3.2 and 3.3).

I want a balance for my students because easy reading builds confidence and hard reading builds skills. Anything that is always hard becomes something I avoid. Ann Patchett (2009) sums it up this way: "I'm all for reading bad books because I consider them to be a gateway drug. People who read bad books now may or may not read better books in the future. People who read nothing now will read nothing in the future."

I don't read only what's good for me. I read junk magazines while getting my haircut each month; I look forward to it. I gather recommendations for romance novels—girl-gets-perfect-man stories—and inhale them in an afternoon. I've read so much truly great literature in my life that some might ask why I bother with a paperback that is only entertainment. It's all about balance—which applies to most things we do. I know I'm not a better person for the hours spent watching *What Not to Wear*, but sometimes I appreciate the break after a day of the serious work of teaching. I tune in so I don't have to think too hard. And yes, our students have this need, too. If we want to create lifelong, satisfied readers, we need a balance between the careful study of complex texts and time to pursue personal passions in books of choice for pure pleasure. The key is we have to *teach* both.

I call it roller coaster reading, and I believe all readers do it. The long, slow climb of a dense and difficult text, followed by something easy, flying through the pages, racing past turns breathless and engaged in the ride. The big climb goes up and up and you feel the pull against the back of your seat it's so steep. (That's a classic novel for most teenagers, even for really good readers.) That feeling of exhilaration at the top—at the end of a climb—should be real. I think all kids deserve that feeling, deserve to slowly make sense of something really difficult, like the *New Yorker* article on capital punishment I'm assigning for homework next week, or *Great Expectations*, which Elizabeth has chosen to read this month. The exhilaration at the top is partially born of the difficulty of the climb. Let's get kids there. But if we're smart, we'll recognize that all readers need the ride down, too. No one I know wants to work all the time. I remember this when I look out at the teenagers in my class whose current interests in reading are a mixture of challenge and ease. I am determined to help my students find a balance in their choices as a prelude to their reading lives once they finish high school. I know that one important thing we can do for struggling readers is help them glide through books they enjoy.

Good Teaching Is Based Not on a System But on a Relationship

You might read this book and think that a system of book talks, conferences, accountability, and text study might change a classroom of readers. I know it won't. It's not about the system.

The most important condition in my classroom is my relationship with my students. My students are not moving through a system that guarantees they'll read; I am moving them through a system that helps me manage the large number of students I teach. The magic formula is the relationship we form and my ability to meet them where they are, accept where they are, and then put books in their hands that will ignite their own intrinsic motivation to read.

I value engagement more than any particular text, and helping students learn to make good choices rests on suggestion, not coercion. I believe the only real and lasting interest in reading comes from engagement, so it is at the heart of what I do. The secret of my system, perhaps, is the accepted and encouraged diversity of the books that line my shelves.

My measurement of success is how students talk about themselves as readers—as self-engaged, curious readers. Like Meaghan did in an essay last spring:

> The worst feeling in the world is starting a new book, opening it up and feeling the entire book on the unread side, and having nothing but the cover in your other hand, or at least I thought so before this year. I thought that this was both intimidating and daunting. I never liked to read before, and I think that a lot of it was because I hated the feeling of starting a new book. After this year however, I am now excited when I open a new book, because I get excited for what is in store for me in my full, right hand.
>
> Before this year, I hated reading. I could never find books that I liked, and I always had better things to do with my time than read. Reading was boring. It was intimidating and important and I figured that it was better to ignore it than to face it. I knew that I was a slow reader and I knew that I needed to work on it, but I never wanted to. I justified my lack of reading by telling myself that I didn't read because I didn't have any good books, but I now know that I never looked very hard either.

In this past year, I have read over twenty books, and I have grown to love reading. I have found books that I am interested in, and I have challenged myself and learned a lot. I think that finding books that I like was one of the best things that could have happened to my education, because reading was something that I was really lacking in. Since the beginning of this year, all of my classes have become easier because it is easier for me to read and comprehend things quicker and more thoroughly.

My favorite books this year were probably *One Amazing Thing, The Curious Incident of the Dog in the Nighttime, Rules,* and *Lost in the Meritocracy. Rules* and *The Curious Incident of the Dog in the Nighttime* were very interesting to me because I want to go into working with people with mental disabilities. *One Amazing Thing* was really good because I love books about people from different backgrounds, and that was exactly what that book was all about. *Lost in the Meritocracy* is very interesting because I know a lot of students, including myself sometimes, who float through school the way that Walter Kirn did, and this book clearly demonstrates why that is not the way to do things. It has caused me to think differently, and I know that that is a path that I never want to go down. I did not like the book *Incendiary*. For some reason it felt really forced to me. For some reason I was not able to get into the plot. I did, however, love *Little Bee* by the same author.

In spending more time reading, I have learned a lot about my own writing. I have found that it is easier to write for myself. It is kind of like having an unending supply of mentor texts. Every time I read something, I notice how it is written and what is different. I think one of the biggest things that I have taken to use in my own writing is that I learned that jumping from topic to topic can still be organized if you do it in the right way. Things don't always have to go in chronological order or flow into each other, because sometimes the jumps and disorganization illustrates the point in a whole new way.

If I could go back and do high school over I would start reading earlier, even before high school. Reading makes everything easier and it is very enjoyable. I never would have guessed that I could learn so much just by reading novels, but I have really learned a lot.

A system will not create readers, but the books that keep a reader seeking will.

If the trajectory in our teaching is focused on lifelong reading as I believe it must be, then I believe we should be moving readers toward greater choice as they age. It just makes sense. Students are more compliant in elementary than in middle school and more compliant in middle than in high school. Yet we narrow their choices to the deep, slow study of a few novels a year in high school, just when their interests are expanding and growing and their potential for consuming many books in a year has reached a peak. Just as students are less likely to trust our choices (because they seek independence and adulthood) and just as the pressure increases on teachers to lower failure and dropout rates (because each course counts toward graduation), we narrow reading to a small number of books that students quickly learn they can fake their way around.

I am not advocating eliminating the study of literature and hope that there will always be a host of choices in the deep study of literature at all ages, but I am questioning the balance between content and kids. The study of literature is a rich experience, but literature study alone cannot offer the volume of reading that professors are after and that employers want. The volume of reading that leads to an informed population at the ballot box. The volume of reading that lasts.

Nudging One Reader

~*~*~

There is in you what is beyond you.

—Paul Valery

I embarrass my children with a pesky habit I have. I fill time with a simple question: *What are you reading?* I ask it in the checkout line at the grocery store, I question the young girl swiping my credit card at J. Crew, I swap titles with Paul at the post office, I query taxi drivers, policemen, business owners, and of course, my children's friends when they stop by our house to visit—many of whom are my former students. I ask for two reasons: one, I want titles I haven't heard of, and two, I want to know if former students are still reading. Like my mentor Don Graves, I am always collecting data, pulling information together that will make me a more effective teacher.

I could tell lots of stories that illuminate the difficulty of moving kids one by one into a life of reading. I have lists in my notebook of students I might write about, but today I settle on Keith. Why? You would instantly like him; I'm sure of it. He arrived in senior English with his rumpled plaid shirt and jeans, his brown hair brushed from the back of his head forward, more like an afterthought than a fashion statement. He never seemed to try hard to be likeable, he just was. He spoke with confidence, laughed easily, and drew other kids in. He was honest, always, but not with the adolescent abrasiveness that too often distances students and teachers. Keith was a happy teenager, content and easy.

I take attendance most mornings by standing at the door to my room as kids arrive, making conversation—"How are you doing? Nice jacket—how's your dog?" You know—the banter that says I noticed your new boots, I'm glad you're here, I like you. Or I stand in front of the door with one of my foam swords from the Globe Theatre and refuse to let students enter without giving me a vocabulary word in a sentence that shows what it means. I'm fierce with a sword in my hand. They groan and complain, but when I challenge them to try to get past my sword, they laugh and play along. Keith would be the first to say, "Aw, Ms. Kittle, I don't know any!" and I'd say, "Guess you're stuck out here today then." We'd both laugh. He'd think, try to peek inside at our board of words and definitions, and I'd whack him with the sword. Sometimes his friend Liam would stand with him, coaching him, rattling off words he should know until Keith would seize on one and come up with a sentence, right at the bell. Cracked me up every time.

I survey students in the first week about their reading habits, interests, and experiences. I get some honest answers about reading; some students hide because they just don't trust me yet. Keith was clear: "Never liked reading, not a reader, not a good writer, but I'll work hard, I promise." I could feel his grin even in his words.

I knew he didn't read much—I could see it when I asked him to find a book to read on the first day of class. He scanned the shelves, chatted with friends, skimmed spines with disinterest, then grabbed a book and went to his seat. He opened it and assumed the posture of a reader: head down, eyes on the page. I scanned the rest of the class. Who pulled books out of bags and who found one on the shelves easily? Who was still avoiding the choice several minutes in? Nonreaders are easy to spot. It's what we teachers do once we notice that matters. My eyes returned to Keith within a minute and he was looking around just like I was. That book he'd chosen held him for thirty seconds at most. I need to remember the challenge of building stamina from nothing. Even if the book is right, reading it is like that first run after years of inactivity—a little, then a little more, until you can glide along for minutes at a time.

Keith was easy. That still bothers me: He was easy to work with, but he hadn't read in years. He was malleable but unprepared to choose college if that became his choice. Why? Lots of reasons, but one stuck out when we talked about it in an early reading conference. He just couldn't make sense of the reading assigned to him in high school. I know he should have had more stamina, he should have "tried harder," but he didn't, so he didn't read. It was too easy for him to get by in all of his classes without it. Keith was a happy but only half-listening student who was not learning enough to be ready for the increasing literacy demands of work or college. He passed his courses without reading much of anything. This shouldn't happen. But it does.

Here's how Keith described September in my room:

> I started off reading *Boot Camp* [by Todd Strasser] the first day and that certainly was a great choice for me. Right after I picked it up, the next day you had a book talk about it and that really got me to stick with it and I'm glad I did. This was my first year ever actually reading one book and liking it. I was hooked from the beginning, which is unheard of. I usually can't get hooked and I always get confused and get lost and end up just throwing it out.

What happens when a reader gets hooked? You know, because it happens to you all the time. But for a student like Keith, the impact was staggering.

Keith had a job and a girlfriend, and he was a starter on our football team, which was expected to play in the state championship that year. Like most teenagers, he didn't see a lot of room in his life for reading. Football is an everyday commitment in the fall, but Keith said he found himself reading every single night. "I remember a game against Plymouth Saturday morning. [Plymouth has been Kennett's most important rival for decades.] I stayed up reading *Boot Camp* until eleven at night instead of getting sleep before the biggest game of the year. By then I realized, wow, I'm starting to like to read."

Students are greedy readers when the book is just right. This one was. Because reading is an everyday expectation in my room—every student moves from one book to the next; some are trained athletes clearing hurdles, others I pursue until we're both exhausted. Sometimes I catch a break, though, when there's a trilogy just about everyone wants to read. Thank you, Suzanne Collins. Keith knew other students were talking about *The Hunger Games*, so he put it on his next list and found it thrilling. "The same thing happened with *Hunger Games*. I would stop playing video games or hanging out with my girlfriend just so I could read those books. I read those books each in a matter of a week because I read every second I could." This practice matters, of course. Just like with football, the only way Keith will improve as a reader is with daily practice.

We moved into the cruelest month for seniors: October. Keith was conflicted about college. The after-graduation decision loomed. Seniors juggle applications, essays, letters of recommendation, visits to campuses, and that measuring of themselves against others' expectations that makes them wince. Keith felt the pressure but was conflicted. His mom wanted him to go to college and he couldn't imagine letting her down, but his father, an electrician, had apprenticed Keith to construction work and Keith loved it. What to do? Even though he was conflicted, I am expected to prepare him for college expectations, should he choose to go.

By the end of first quarter Keith wrote, "I've read over 1,000 pages, which is ridiculous." We celebrated. I started greeting him in the morning with something stupid and uncool like, "How's my reading Jedi Master?" He would grin, roll his eyes, and shake his head, but he was pleased. I wanted to live there with him in the land of discovery. There are so many good books. But I also wanted more than easy books for him. I felt the pressure of time: how to prepare a nonreader for college reading in eighteen weeks? I didn't want him to lose his passion or his newly acquired reading habit, so this is where it became formidable for both of us. I suggested challenging books and he ignored me. I persisted. He hesitated. I gave a book talk on *The Book Thief*, by Markus Zusak. It went on his next list. When I asked why, he told me that Death as a narrator sounded pretty cool. Excellent.

Keith began *The Book Thief* slowly. I expected it. I read and reread the first time I began the book. It requires a reader's full attention. More than that, it releases bits of information, asking readers to connect images and ideas to what they know about World War II and Germany and the human sacrifices in war. Keith wanted the challenge, but was he ready for it? I'm not sure. I think I pushed too hard. Keith had only been living the reading life for about ten weeks, and I think his confidence needed more support before he was ready to struggle again. His practiced response was giving up, but that would be a cursed strategy in college. I didn't look for a book close in difficulty to the ones he'd finished, which I regret. I let him choose based on interest, expecting that his engagement and Zusak's masterful storytelling would keep him turning pages, even if at a slower pace. And I was right—for about three weeks. Keith was more than two thirds of the way in when he finally abandoned the book. He wrote,

"*The Book Thief* is definitely a good book, but not for me. It just was the same old thing every day and a very long book. I'm sure it's a great book for some people, but not for me." He traded it for *A Long Way Gone,* by Ishmael Beah, and became immersed again, finishing the book in just over two weeks.

I think abandoning books is a life lesson, not a failure. Surely the student who always abandons books needs support to find success, but students who read for hundreds of pages and then decide to trade the book for something else may miss the end of one book but are thinking critically about their reading and making a choice. All readers do this. Keith swapped a book he had lost interest in reading for another book and kept reading, which is not a failure to me. He didn't turn to SparkNotes or another cheating route to pretend he was reading, he simply chose a book from his next list and began again.

Keith rode the wave of nightly reading until the end of the semester, surprising us both with how it impacted his writing. "The biggest thing I picked up on was dialogue in books. I started reading more and seeing the punctuation. I was not good with punctuation and I think this year I greatly improved. . . . Writing has taught me to look at reading differently. Now I read and can break it down and I know so many more words from vocabulary study that I actually have seen in my books so I can understand." These are important things, but what struck me came at the end of his reflection. "Most importantly this class allowed me to think and think really hard. What makes good writing is what comes from the soul. When someone lets out their emotions or what they really believe in or what they have locked up inside their head or someone's imagination spilt out onto a piece of white lined paper, that makes good writing. Good writing is someone's strong belief in something and why they believe in it. I define good writing [as,] if you can tell the person has facts or evidence or just thoughts to back it up."

I pulled Keith out into the hall at the close of the semester and turned on my video camera. I asked him, "In your four years of high school, I want to know how many books you have read."

"My four years of high school, well"—his eyes scanned the ceiling—"I read about seven this year, so I'm going to have to say about eight." Big smile.

There are so many ways to respond to that truth. Do I celebrate the seven he read in one semester in my class or dig into the prior three years? This day I wanted to understand why so many kids won't read what we assign to them. There was hesitation in my voice as I asked, "So what did you read in ninth, tenth, and eleventh grade?"

I hesitated because my interviews have sometimes felt like investigative reporting on my colleagues. It isn't my intent, and the staff has turned over many times in the fifteen years I've been teaching in Conway, so there isn't a direct correlation between the new teachers I've mentored and the students in my room. My colleagues are excellent. They are. Still, it is disturbing how few books kids have read when they enter my room after a steady diet of classic texts, even taught by enthusiastic, committed teachers. So I asked.

Keith looked a little embarrassed. "I don't think I read anything." He eyed the ceiling again. "I skimmed read, SparkNoted a little bit." He blanched at the term *SparkNoted*, as if he knew it was distasteful, but he had to own it.

I asked him why he didn't read, because some students surprise me with answers I haven't considered. His wasn't one of them, though. Keith directed his gaze right at the camera, "Laziness." After a brief pause he added, "And I don't like reading." He leaned back against dark blue lockers for a fraction of a second before adding, "I do now, though. But I didn't like the books that they gave us."

I've thought a lot about why kids won't try. It's an important question. It isn't only because there are easy ways to cheat. Keith told me he always tried to read the assigned reading. He was serious, intense. "But I just couldn't do it. I'd read ten pages, but I wouldn't understand anything. I wouldn't get anything out of it. I couldn't interpret what it was saying—it was like I was brain-dead." He thought for a minute. "It was just blank. I realized at the end of the ten pages, I'm like I don't remember anything. So then I just gave up." No one wants to be defeated by reading, or worse, to admit it and ask for help. I wish this wasn't true, but I know it is. Many nonreaders fumble along in school without working on the very thing they need to overcome their struggle: reading.

"I don't really remember reading any—even one book." He smiled, and then looked away. Truth isn't easy. Keith was good at so many things. No doubt his inability to make sense of what was given to him to read in high school frustrated him. And this is where teaching can make such a difference, but only if we're helping students become stronger independent readers, not simply summarizing or interpreting the text for them.

Keith showed me again the power in what I believe is our only chance with nonreaders—get them reading. Until they're turning pages independently, they won't apply what we teach them in close reading. Guided practice with texts isn't enough; students need daily independent practice. We have to expect more: expect more reading and then expect more difficult reading. The supports have to increase as the challenge of the reading does, but that is the teaching I rise to. I relish helping students unravel a most difficult text. I expect each student to gain the facility to make sense of reading that once felt out of reach. It is that hope that pulls me through the hardest days of connecting discouraged readers to books.

This is the calling of an English teacher for me: give each student books that teach them, challenge them, and lead them to places they'll never know otherwise. Take them across the world on a journey of thought. Make every student think, and think really hard, as Keith said. Lead them to see books as allies, not enemies. Years later when you call for an electrician and Keith answers the phone, ask him what he's reading and he'll have an answer.

Keith chose to enter the construction business in heating and cooling systems, but soon discovered he needed a college degree for the work, which his company is paying for.

In my notebook I seek connections between independent reading and mentor text study.

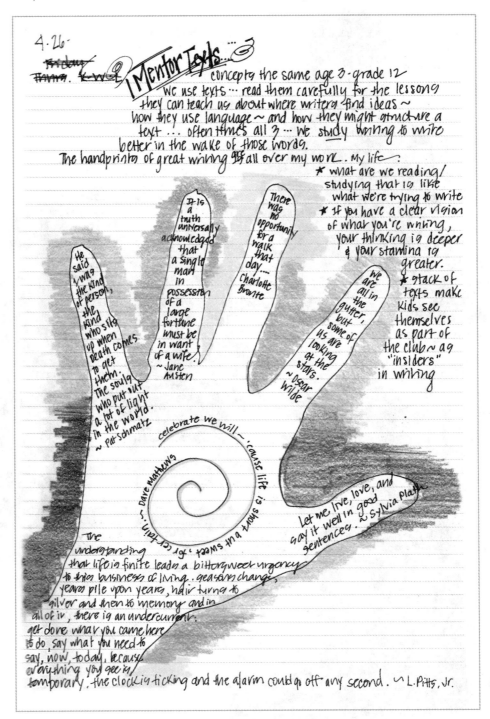

4.26.

① Mentor Texts...

concepts the same age 3 - grade 12
We use texts ... read them carefully for the lesson
they can teach us about where writers find ideas ~
how they use language ~ and how they might structure a
text ... often times all 3 ... we study wanting to write
better in the wake of those words.
The handprints of great writing are all over my work. My life :

★ what are we reading/
studying that is like
what we're trying to write
★ If you have a clear vision
of what you're writing,
your thinking is deeper
& your stamina is
greater.
★ stack of
texts make
kids see
themselves
as part of
the club ~ as
"insiders"
in writing

He said I was the kind of person, the kind who sits up when death comes to get them. The souls who put out a lot of light in the world. ~ Pat Schmatz

It is a truth universally acknowledged that a single man in possession of a large fortune must be in want of a wife. ~ Jane Austen

There was no opportunity for a walk that day.... Charlotte Bronte

We are all in the gutter, but some of us are looking at the stars. ~ Oscar Wilde

celebrate we will ~ cause life is short but sweet, for certain. ~ Dave Matthews

Let me live, love, and say it well in good sentences. ~ Sylvia Plath

The understanding that life is finite leads a bittersweet urgency to the business of living. seasons change, years pile upon years, hair turns to silver and then to memory and in all of it, there is an undercurrent. get done what you came here to do, say what you need to say, now, today, because everything you see is temporary. the clock is ticking and the alarm could go off any second. ~ L. Pitts, Jr.

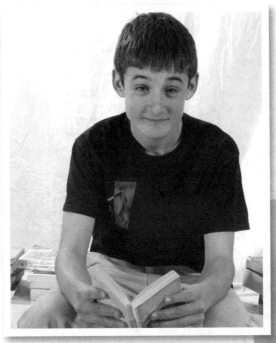

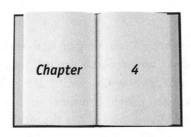

Chapter   **4**

Opening Doors into Reading

When the young see their teacher excited about books that include families and homes like the students', they connect more deeply with themselves, with us, and with the text.

—*Pat Mora*

I call most assigned reading the *narrow door* into a reading life. We choose hard books, and for many, they are intimidating. This door, like the gated entrance to servants' quarters near Prague Castle, in the Czech Republic (see Figure 4.1), opens on stairs that are steep and take you up a dark stairwell that prevents you from seeing where you are going most of the time. There's a beautiful view at the top, but getting there is arduous and only some will make it. We try to convince students that all the work they put into assigned reading will be worth it, but it is hard to lead and keep track of all our students at the same time, so some of them will fall behind in the reading and decide to give up. This stairway is crumbling from years of use, but just because it's old doesn't mean there isn't a lot to learn by climbing it. Still, when I have students use it, I know I will lose some along the way.

Figure 4.1 *Prague Castle*

Figure 4.2 *Bunratty Castle*

Luckily it isn't the only way in. We can reach the breathtaking, mind-altering views of literature through many doors. Bunratty Castle, in Ireland, near Shannon (see Figure 4.2) represents the *door of resilience*. It seems to rise from nowhere, as if it remains here two hundred years later due to its inner strength. It is beautiful, though, as tough things often are. Similarly, resilient stories stand against impossible odds. They inspire. Books about resilience can be a good fit for a reader who is looking for characters and situations that will help him imagine standing up against the impossible things in his own life. I recommend *Head Case*, by Sarah Aronso; *Hate List*, by Jennifer Brown; *A Heartbreaking Work of Staggering Genius*, by Dave Eggers; *They Poured Fire on Us from the Sky*, by Benjamin Ajak, Benson Deng, and Alephonsian Deng; *The Other Wes Moore*, by Wes Moore; *Makes Me Wanna Holler*, by Nathan McCall; and *Extremely Loud and Incredibly Close*, by Jonathan Safran Foer. For nonfiction readers, consider *Behind the Beautiful Forevers*, by Katherine Boo, which is set inside the slums of Mumbai.

You might say, but almost all of the books you've listed are long, challenging texts. They are. In this chapter I want you to think about reluctant readers not only as those with low skills but also as those who have the skills and yet are looking for a reason to read. We need a wide mix of texts at different ability levels that are inviting, intoxicating, and available.

Figure 4.3 *View from Castle in Ireland*

The ruins in Figure 4.3, seen from a cemetery in Ireland, represent the door of *courage*. To restore this place would take courage; it's abandoned, defeated, the rubble of its former self. This is the door you wish you didn't have to walk through, but somehow you do, and you start over. I know books that tell stories of strength in the face of pain or grief. I know characters who face what frightens them. These books may inspire teenagers you know to face the worst with courage.

Students tell me that stories of courage hide within books about family and life in high school. Think about a young man raising a new baby by himself in *The First Part Last*, by Angela Johnson, or popular books from the "death and dying" section of my library in which teens wrestle with their own mortality: *Deadline*, by Chris Crutcher, *Hold Still*, by Nina LaCour, and *Forever Changes*, by Brendan Halpin. Don't miss *Willow*, by Julia Hoben, and *Wintergirls*,

Figure 4.4 *Castle near Dublin, Ireland*

by Laurie Halse Anderson, for courageous, unstoppable young women. All these titles appear on lists of students' favorites at the end of the year. Why? Because we all wonder how we might face danger to ourselves or to those we love. Books let us walk through our deepest fears and emerge on the other side. In books we can imagine strength.

The wide, open door to the Irish castle in Figure 4.4 is the *door of invitation*. One example is narrative poetry; it invites you in. Stories told in verse get to the heart of what's happening with few words. Some read like tweets of a larger story, little bits that move the most resistant or the least skilled to feel success as pages turn. My students love everything by Ellen Hopkins, as well as *Because I Am Furniture*, by Thalia Chaltas, *Sold*, by Patricia McCormick, and *Shark Girl*, by Kelly Bingham.

Graphic novels are also inviting. Although they are complex and often have vocabulary that boosts the reading level higher than we expect, the art allows students, especially those who struggle to create a mental picture as they read, to follow the meaning more easily. I love *The Complete Persepolis*, by Marjane Satrapi, *Blankets*, by Craig Thompson, *My Mommy Is in America and She Met Buffalo Bill*, by Jean Regnaud, *Stitches*, by David Small, and *A.D.: New Orleans After the Deluge*, by Josh Neufeld. The *Maus* books, of course, are classic favorites. If you've never read one, you must.

The beautiful door in the interior of Prague Castle shown in Figure 4.5 represents the deep attachment of *love*. Teenagers seek an understanding of love in all its frames.

Figure 4.5 *Interior of Castle in Prague*

They want romance, yes, but they also seek stories about sibling and other family attachments and books that explore the changing love of friendships. *Memoirs of a Teenage Amnesiac*, by Gabrielle Zevin, is the classic girl-with-the-wrong-boy story, with a dramatic and funny twist. *Rules*, by Cynthia Lord, shows the hard work of loving an autistic sibling. *The Art of Racing in the Rain*, by Garth Stein, and *Following Atticus*, by Tom Ryan, show dog love with great beauty, and *Before I Die*, by Jenny Downham, takes you to the heart of what makes us all human. There's even *Delirium*, by Lauren Oliver, to show you love in a dystopian world. It is part of a series, which many readers love. This category is wide and deep. Every year my list expands as students share the books that taught them about love. Someday, I swear, I'll write my own.

The gate to the gardens of Arundel Castle, in Scotland (see Figure 4.6), represents *acceptance*. Students seek an understanding of themselves and others. Acceptance brings peace. I think of *North of Beautiful*, by Justina Chen Headley, a brave story of a girl who must accept the port-wine-colored stain across her face that her father cannot, or the incomparable Doug in *Okay for Now*, by Gary Schmidt, who learns to accept his family and his fate and then must accept his best friend's as well. *Shine*, by Lauren Myracle, requires readers to accept the brutal consequences of hate, and *Letters from a Dead Girl*, by Jo Knowles, brings a young girl to terms with a destructive, abusive friendship. For the many students in foster care, *One for the Murphys*, by Lynda Mullaly Hunt, is a moving

Figure 4.6 *Arundel Castle Gardens, Scotland*

portrait of possibility and love, while also showing the realities of broken circumstances and damaged relationships.

Humor is an important door (see Figure 4.7). So many young men have finally trusted me with regard to books simply because I found one that made them laugh. Try *Knucklehead*, by Jon Scieszka, or *Dead End in Norvelt*, by Jack Gantos. *A Walk in the Woods*, by Bill Bryson, is almost a sure thing: after they read it, they want to read all of his books. My students also like *Slam*, by Nick Hornby, and *The Book of Guy Stories*, by Garrison Keillor.

History and war (see Figure 4.8) are doors for many young readers who seek knowledge, not stories. They get both, of course, but these are purposeful readers who want to leave a book wiser than when they opened it, and wiser with facts, not just experiences. This section of my library is filled primarily with adult nonfiction and memoir. From *War*, by Sebastian Junger, to *The Good Soldiers*, by David Finkel, from *Blood and Thunder*, *Hellhound on His Trail*, and *Ghost Soldiers*, by Hampton Sides, to realistic fiction like *March*, by Geraldine Brooks, *Sunrise Over Fallujah*, by Walter Dean Myers, *Forge*, by Laurie Halse Anderson, and *Copper Sun*, by Sharon Draper. I seek the best fiction and nonfiction available to keep readers satisfied.

Nearby (Figure 4.9) is a door I call simply *biography*. It lets you into a world you couldn't imagine before. Try a few years in a maximum-security prison like *Hole in My Life*, by Jack Gantos, or *A Place to Stand*, by Jimmy Santiago Bacca, or *Fish*, by T. J. Parsell. Enter the world of mental illness beside Ned Vizzini in *It's Kind of a Funny Story* or walk beside boy soldier Ishmael Beah in *A Long Way Gone*. This section includes autobiographies, biographies about historical figures, and the "as told to" life stories of celebrities and sports figures. I'm not sure there is a clear distinction between memoir, creative nonfiction, and autobiography. All tell life stories. Many of my students become readers because they pick up a book by a famous wrestler, NASCAR driver, football player, or comedian. I say, whatever it takes.

Some students seek escape through *fantasy*. The door in Figure 4.10 is the entrance to The Elephant House, in Edinburg, Scotland, where J. K. Rowling famously composed the first Harry Potter book. My family and I sat at

Figure 4.7 *Irish Castle and My Son, Cam Kittle*

Figure 4.8 *Chichen Itza*

Figure 4.9 *Arundel Castle, Scotland*

Figure 4.10 *The Elephant House, Edinburg, Scotland, Where J. K. Rowling Composed* Harry Potter

the table where she worked, looking out toward Edinburg Castle, imagining her writing process. (You might have figured out by now that we're an odd family.) *The Hunger Games*, by Suzanne Collins, is here, of course, beside *The Astonishing Life of Octavian Nothing: Traitor to the Nation*, by M. T. Anderson, *How I Live Now*, by Meg Rosoff, and the incredible new collection of short stories from fourteen authors you and your students love (Stephen King, Jon Scieszka, Kate DiCamillo, Sherman Alexie, among others) called *The Chronicles of Harris Burdick*. I also found myself swept away by the beauty of words in *Breadcrumbs*, by Anne Ursu.

Of course there are doors I haven't mentioned. Many teens have found reading lives through a bloody door opened by a love-struck vampire or behind a bolted one masking pure terror and gore. I don't read books about serial killers and mayhem, but I have students who do. Stories that scare me, like *Stolen*, by Lucy Christopher, in which a sixteen-year-old girl is kidnapped in the Bangkok airport just steps away from her parents, or *Girl, Stolen*, by April Henry, in which a car is jacked with a blind teenager in the back seat, keep me up at night as it is. Try *After*, by Amy Efaw, in which a high school athlete delivers a baby in the bathroom and tosses it in a dumpster after months of denial, or *Before I Fall*, by Lauren Oliver, in which you are forced to relive a deadly car accident, again and again, as the central character tries to heal her past. They are as unsettling as they are captivating. They grab readers and demand they keep going. That's an entry into reading that just might last.

More titles appear every time I look. (I post reading lists on my website if you're looking for more.) We all have a lot of reading to do. I can't wait.

What About Balance?

A teacher was seated in the front row of my workshop. He had pen ready, paper in front of him, handouts nearby. He was attentive. That's why his hand shot straight up after we watched a video of a student telling the story of not reading in ninth, tenth, and eleventh grades and then reading sixteen books during senior year. His question didn't surprise me. "What about balance?!" he nearly shouted. "They can't be reading those easy books as seniors!"

If there were evidence that determining everything students *should* read at each grade level produced successful independent reading year after year, I would understand why English teachers get so frustrated with what I'm suggesting here. But there is so much evidence that kids aren't reading in high school. Controlling what students read stifles readers. Dick Allington (2001) has said, "I know of no evidence that suggests that any curriculum plan that had all children working in the same books all day, all week, all year, ever produced high achievement in all children, or even in most children" (118).

I believe that crafting an individual reading life of challenge, whim, curiosity and hunger is the most important thing for each of my students to achieve. It is as important for Meaghan, an honors student headed toward a selective college and serious study as a humanities major, as it is for Alex, who will become a landscaper when he graduates and hopes never to attend college. It is not too late to lead a nonreader to reading in high school. It's never too late. It can happen with a senior. It can happen with every student. It might not in the year I have him or her, but if we all focus on this, it will happen.

Kids want to read stories that surprise and challenge them. They want to dig into nonfiction and become an expert on World War II or a person they're interested in, and when they do, they are practicing all the reading skills we want them to leave high school with. They will be able to challenge shallow and deceitful thinking, be it in advertising or the news. They will own the joy of reading and be determined to pass it on to their own children. They will be able to access a warehouse of knowledge even if they can't afford college. They will be able to read *To Kill a Mockingbird* when they want to read it.

Consider the reading we need to balance during a yearlong English class:

1. We need to study literature (whole texts).
2. We need to read short mentor texts (in all genres) to understand the writer's craft and create a vision for what we ourselves will write.
3. We need to develop an independent reading life.

(I know there are other things we'll be doing, like increasing our focus on digital literacies and speaking and listening, but I'm concerned here with how well we are balancing reading in our teaching.)

When I first sat down a dozen years ago and charted the time I spent on literature versus independent reading in a month of my teaching, I was surprised at how out of balance it was. Literature study was at the center, and everything else was a satellite. Achievement for some of the students in my English class almost certainly represented compliance, not ability. And this was serious. This had consequences that hurt my students. Parents saw a B on the report card and believed their student was prepared for college-level reading. The course was college prep and the grade was above average, so the student thought, I can do this. What else would he conclude? Yet a student with a B average in English could slip by without reading a single book.

He would in no way be prepared for college reading. I know conditions in many schools are ridiculous. I know when I had 175 seventh graders each day many of them successfully faked the required reading. I couldn't keep on top of it all.

You may not be able to either, but if you focus on creating readers, you'll find that you'll have a whole lot more of them. If this country wants to get serious about education as empowering and life changing, we need reasonable class sizes in middle and high school. But since we haven't achieved this yet, and there are no signs that we will soon, I just keep trying to do the best I can with what I have. And the best I can do is not let fake-reading go by unnoticed.

Here's my formula for balanced reading in an English course: independent reading—increasing challenge and complexity over time, meeting goals, reflecting, studying short texts in class (including many commonly required, like "Letter from a Birmingham Jail," by Martin Luther King Jr.)—50 percent; annotating thinking of mentor texts and using those lessons to write better in the genre—25 percent; and whole-class or small-group novel study—25 percent. This is close to Allington's suggestion: "While school plans might have some common texts that all students use, my advice is that common texts—single-source lessons—be used no more than 20–30 percent of the time. And when common texts are used, teachers must still adapt instruction so that these texts are accessible to all students" (2001, 118).

Building a Classroom Library

In my first years at our old high school, I was a traveling teacher, used to being an invader of another teacher's space with no real rights. I was in the math portable classroom one hour, in the Spanish teacher's portable the next, then camped out in the social studies department chair's room in the main building. But I still felt lucky, because I had colleagues in much worse conditions. I wasn't assigned to teach journalism in the wood shop, for example, or business education in the room behind the auto shop where I had to breathe gas fumes all day. School can be a tough place: the classroom environment matters (it's 25 percent of my school district's performance evaluation), but I had little control over mine. I remembered my room in the middle school with longing and regret. It was mine all day, every day. I made it beautiful.

Finally one year we were given a writing lab in Don Graves' name, a gift from a lifetime educator in our valley who was passionate about providing opportunities for students. It wasn't hard—we simply took a classroom and added desktop computers—but the revolutionary part was its designation as English only. It was a space, finally, that English teachers could count on. I was allowed to teach there one period a day, and I worked hard to maintain it.

I knew I needed a classroom library. My colleague Ed Fayle had been making time for reading in his writing classes, and we often discussed how critical it was that students discover a love of books. Ed made it happen, and I followed. I was assigned a section of writing with seniors, and I placed reading at the center of the course. Problem was, my fifty or so titles, culled from my personal library and the English department book room, quickly disappeared into the hands of students. I needed many more. I didn't know how many more in the beginning, and I'm glad I didn't, because I might have given up before I started.

Building a classroom library became my mission. There's no magical formula for the accumulation: you start reading and begging and spending money. With luck you'll find some sources of funds other than your own checkbook, like school and district monies, but don't neglect used-book stores, friends, and former students who are moving beyond the titles they loved in the past. Our school has boxes for donations from parents and community members. I visit the library sales in the summer. A teacher I know in Indianapolis sent out a mass email begging friends for castoffs and her room went from some to tons. Whatever works, do it. Books, books, and more books. It is magical, in a way I'll never fully understand, but my students began reading volumes more once books began to line the shelves around us.

There is a letter to parents about our independent reading program posted on my website. I explain that I can't read everything students choose to read and I often don't remember the details of books I've read. I ask them to please let me know if the content of books their child reads is a great concern, so we can work together on the choices. I ask parents and students to sign a statement saying they understand books are not banned in my room and some content may be offensive to some. But I also believe something Ann Patchett (2009) says: "Some children were lucky enough to have their Potter novels banned by witch-hunting school boards and micromanaging ministers. Is there any greater joy than a book you're not allowed to read, a book you could go to hell for reading?"

Students want to read books on the edge. It is the nature of adolescents to want to press us, but there are books I choose not to keep in my library. As Donalyn Miller (2012) says, we are curators of classroom libraries, not just collectors. For example, a popular college-party-life book is a must-read among seniors this year, but when students add it to the title wish list, I tell them why I won't order it. I've skimmed it and know it will be offensive to many. More important, it's not good writing. I can't justify tax dollars (or my own) spent on it. But that doesn't mean I won't let students read it. That book might be the door that leads a kid into reading. You have to make decisions about books based on your community and your school. I suggest being open with parents and administrators about the books in your classroom library, clearly stating why you believe choice matters, and then reading as many of the titles as you can, so you know what you are handing to a student.

I also believe that student agency matters. My students curate the library with me. We discuss the range of books I've collected and what is missing. Students frequently add titles to the order list and advocate for authors I don't know.

I leave you with what Ellen Hopkins (2012), author of many books my students devour, including the *Crank* trilogy, has said about censorship:

> Now let's take a look at the most frequently challenged books for the past three years. What topics do they address? Sexuality. Gender identity. Physical, mental, and sexual abuse. Drugs. Race and racism. Religion. Diversity. The same issues that are being scrubbed or excised from schools, textbooks, discussions and, should certain special interests succeed, our society as a whole.
>
> But these are human truths. They are facets of our vibrant cultural landscape and must be embraced, not denied. It is vital that our children are raised with empathy, knowledge, and understanding of those who are different, yes, but also of themselves. To realize that diversity enriches us. That addiction steals from us. That sexuality is born in us. That gender identity is programmed into our genes. That every one of us is as important as the next, and our differences should be celebrated because each of us holds inside a unique contribution to the greater good.
>
> History illustrates these things, and sheds light on them through perspective. But history is being sanitized, rewritten. Educators can teach these things. But teachers are being silenced. Parents can initiate these discussions. But many parents are afraid, ignorant of the facts themselves, or just too busy to talk to their children. Without books that open minds, through fictional portraits or real, our young people may never have the information they need to make sound decisions or overcome irrational fears. And to disallow books about other cultures or identities is to marginalize and devalue them, or even pretend they don't exist. This is at the heart of bullying. Violence. War.
>
> We cannot allow narrow interest groups to halt our forward movement toward a time when every human life is valued. We need more books like those that top the most challenged lists. We must address those challenges with logic that dissolves the fear driving them. It is essential that we keep those books on bookshelves, so

they can feed the imaginations and open the minds and hearts of our youth. Our children are the future. And it will be a grim future, indeed, if the advocates of regression are allowed to accomplish their goals.

Maintaining a Classroom Library

I wish I could say I've figured this out by now. There's the obvious part: having students help organize the books in a way that is most useful to them. I gave up ABC order by author's last name a few years back and now organize them by themes my students have identified so that they can more easily find books without my help. My students and I also pitch in and reshelve books; it's second nature. I like touching the books, remembering the stories within as I gather my thinking at the end of a day.

The less obvious and more critical part is how I can get students to return the books they borrow. I've tried every conceivable checkout system. They work for some of my students; others would rather sneak books out of the room. Even students who don't have me as a teacher come in between classes and look for books. "Who are you?" I'll ask, then watch a nimble ninth grader dart out between the entering seniors. I shout, "Stop! Give me that book back!" But, really, is that who I want to be? Sometimes, I'm afraid the answer is yes. When there is scarcity, people behave badly. I consider using one of those potions Gretchen Bernabei gave me when NCTE was in San Antonio. According to the directions, if I sprinkle a few drops of a murky liquid at the classroom door, their hands will turn green or they'll itch all over if they steal a book.

I hate this truth about teenagers: some will return everything they borrow, and some will leave my beautiful books under the seats of their cars with the decaying French fries. I put my name along the trimmed edge of a closed book in permanent marker and promise students that my spirit will haunt them forever if they keep one of my books, but I've lost so many titles that I realize there just isn't an answer. I want to beat my head against those empty shelves, but there's no way to fix it. I will reorder the entire set of "death and dying" books again this summer, because students connect so deeply with these titles that they spirit them away to read again and again. I can live with that. Sort of. I have to.

I imagine a President of the United States who mandates books for all. As many as you need, he or she will say. I begged for this in a letter I posted on the English Companion Ning (www.englishcompanion.ning.com) one recent spring when I was working on a multigenre project with my students, but President Obama has not replied. I'm still waiting. Meanwhile, I'll be shopping sales and sorting through boxes at yard sales that crop up along the highways in New England after Memorial Day. Meanwhile, I'll just keep buying. And begging. Meanwhile, my students and I will be reading.

My Daily Reading/Writing Workshop

My school now operates on a block schedule, so I see each of my classes every other day for 80 minutes. I have a template in my mind when I plan each day:

1. Welcome and agenda review (what we're learning, how, and why) (2 minutes).
2. Book talk (3–4 minutes).
3. Time to read and confer (10–15 minutes).
4. Notebook work relative to one of the following (10–15 minutes):
   a. Read, write, and revise in response to poetry or other text.
   b. Practice reading strategies with a difficult short text.
   c. Sentence study and imitation.
   d. Mentor text study and response.
   e. Class conference on a draft or other writing group work.
5. Time to craft writing and confer with writers *or* time to reread, write about, and discuss a whole-class text (30–40 minutes).
6. Closure: sharing lines, exit slips, or other gathering and reflecting activities (3–4 minutes).

Of course these elements vary and are adapted to students' needs. There are times when we spend twenty minutes on a rich mentor text, then get so wrapped up in crafting and conferring there's no time left for closure. I never skip the book talk, but when students are deep into writing and revising with a deadline near, we cut out notebook work. There are also days when notebook writing rolls along with such momentum that I can't cut it short. Altering our plans in response to what is happening in the classroom is the art of teaching. I know what is most important: students need to be reading and writing more than they need to be listening to me talking.

My planning template adjusts with the flow of the unit. At the beginning of a genre study, we read and analyze a lot of mentor texts, swimming in what we'll soon be crafting ourselves. Students are still considering topics. They may need a few days to let topics percolate while they are driving to school or waiting for chemistry class to start, so I spend more time on sentence work, quick writing, and daily revision. As students get to drafts, I extend the time to craft and confer and spend more time with individuals. Conferences—both reading and writing—are at the heart of workshop teaching. I have detailed the elements of writing workshop in *Write Beside Them* (2008), so I will not do so here. I teach reading and writing as interdependent processes. My goal is to lead students to find writing lessons in their independent reading and then produce texts that bear the mark of their extensive reading.

Chapter 5

The Power of the Book Talk

Sell It Like You Mean It

As someone who always has thirty books stacked in my office and beside my bed and beside the dog's bed that I'm meaning to read, it's easy to forget that other people don't know what to choose. They walk into a bookstore and feel utterly lost in the face of all those titles, and so they walk out empty-handed.

—*Ann Patchett*

I learned the term *book talk* from Nancie Atwell (2007). I usually talk about four or five books a day during the first week of school because I want to put a lot of titles out there. I need to help the many students who will struggle to find a book at first. I expect students will keep a list of what they want to read next on the last page of their writing notebooks. I check for this every time I read their notebooks.

Students comply more at the start of the year than later—you know, that small window when students still want to impress their new teacher—so I seize it. Every student starts the year with a next list. I say, "Each day I will talk about books that I hope might interest you. Your job is to record the title of a book that you might consider reading. This isn't a commitment. It's a place to go when you finish one book and are looking for the next. And I know that for some of you 'finish one book' sounds like a fantasy, but every student reads in my room. I quote my wise friend Donalyn Miller when I say to you: 'Not reading is not an option. I expect my students to read every day and to read a large volume of books.' I think I can help you find books that you will say are worth reading if you'll give me a chance. So, give the last page in your notebook a title like 'books for the future' or 'possible reads,' what I will call your 'to-read-next list,' and as I'm talking about books today and tomorrow and every day, you'll write down the title if it sounds like it might be a fit for you."

Now is the time to be the master salesman. I think of my dad, who sold cars for most of his life. He was smooth. He made me want to buy cars I wouldn't look at twice when they zipped by on the street. He'd smile and say, "Can I make you a deal?" And then he'd put all his skills to use.

Book Talk Essentials

Hold the book. I check it out from our school library or pull it off the shelf in my classroom. I hold it so kids can see the number of pages and the cover.

Know the book. I have read it (usually), but if I haven't, I'll say why I chose to introduce it when I haven't read it yet. It might be the newest release from an author that I love or I know students love. Or someone I trust sold me on it. I briefly summarize its theme, central conflict, or other details in a minute or so, like a taste test. I connect the book to other books in my library: "If you like death-and-dying books, this one is probably for you." Or: "All action, fast plot, the kind that makes your heart race." Or: "If you like Sherman Alexie, then you'll love Jimmy Santiago Baca."

Read a short passage. I preface this by saying, "I think it helps for you to hear a little bit of the text. See if the narrator's voice appeals to you. Listen to see if this sounds like a book you can see yourself reading." I always select the passage ahead of time, and I try to find a place where the action is heated or the prose is breathtaking or the voice comes through with intensity (like the "10 Things They Don't Teach You About High School" in *Speak*, by Laurie Halse Anderson). It's critical that I read this slowly, with emphasis and clarity. When I skip this part because I didn't prepare ahead of time and there's so much to do that day, fewer kids choose the book. Hearing the voice of a text sells the book and sells kids on reading.

Keep records. I walk to the back of the room where there is a poster labeled *Book Talks* near our library. I write down the title and author on this list and return the book to the shelf or put it on the table to go back to the library. Some teachers tell me they copy effective book passages onto note cards, which they can then use in the following years, which is smart—but I've never managed to be that organized.

Accept help. Students, parents, fellow teachers, librarians, bookstore owners, and even administrators can be good sources for book talks. You are not in this alone. There are book trailers (created by both authors and publishers) on YouTube, and some include quick talks with the author. But you do have to know books and talk about them. If you're not leading from your own reading life, not many students will follow.

Remember how important you are. Your passion is contagious. As Samantha Bennett (2011) wrote on her blog recently, "Sharing things with kids that delight us, make our eyes light up and our brains cackle and our hearts grow bigger, should be the learning target every day. Don't dumb it down . . . make it into the miraculous event it is, every time. Every single time you find a book that moves you, it is a tiny miracle."

But it won't always be you.

As the year moves forward, you can release responsibility for elements of the workshop to your students. Students in my room bring in poems for quick-writing, create their own slam poetry to share, often take over book talks, and suggest great sentences to study. Becoming a community of readers and writers invites the participation of all; I know that students are developing reading lives when their to-read-next lists are filled with books I've never heard of. I want students who listen for recommendations anywhere, from anyone, and record them, students who don't depend on me to lead them. I know how short my time with them is.

Example of a Book Talk

[*there is a trailer for this book on my website that I composed
in front of students as a model of how to create one*]

"I want to tell you about *Why We Broke Up*, by Daniel Handler, with art by Maria Kalman. And with this book, I have to show you just how unusual it is, with watercolors to divide the sections of the story. Look at the back cover—there are quotes from all kinds of authors on heartbreaks they've experienced, which I found pretty entertaining.

"I started this book on Friday and kept finding reasons why I needed to keep reading. By Saturday morning I wrote this in my notebook: 'Today I have the usual list of all that must get done and won't, and this is just one more stupid distraction, but right now it is all I can see: this book—its beautifully crafted sentences and mostly its truth.' I finished the book soon after I wrote that.

"I remain intrigued by this book's construction and the vividness of the details. All these dog-eared pages contain sentences I want to read again and again. There is art and craft here, not just story. No wonder it's one of four 2012 Michael L. Printz honor books, an award recognizing the best writing in young adult literature.

"So here's the story. Min is writing Ed a letter explaining why they have broken up, which she will include in a box of things she's saved from their relationship. Her best friend is driving her to his house to dump the box onto his doorstep. The story itself is predictable, but I still found myself craving the details of how this one relationship unraveled.

"Here's a sample passage describing high school from early in the book:

> It was the bells too loud or rattly in broken speakers that would never get fixed. It was the bad floors squeaky and footprinted, and the bang of lockers. It was writing my name in the upper right-hand corner of the paper or Mr. Nelson would automatically deduct five points, and in the upper left-hand corner of the paper or Mr. Peters would deduct three. It was the pen just giving up midway and scratching invisible ink scars on the paper or suiciding to leak on my hand, and trying to remember if I'd touched my face recently and am I a ballpoint coal miner on my cheeks and chin. It was boys in a fight by the garbage cans for whatever reason, not my friends, not my crowd, my old locker partner crying about it on the bench I sat on freshman year with a gang I barely see anymore. Quizzes, pop quizzes, switching identities during attendance when there's a sub, anything to pass time, more bells. . . . It was the days the sun wasn't even trying to get out of the clouds and be nice for once in its starry life. It was wet grass, damp hems, the wrong socks I forgot to throw out and so now found myself wearing, the sneaky leaf falling from my hair where it had nested for hours to surely someone's delight. . . . Locker combinations, vending machines, hooking up, cutting class, the secrets of smoking and headphones and rum in a soda bottle with mints to cover the breath, that one sickly boy with thick glasses and an electronic wheelchair, thank God I'm not him, or the neck brace, or the rash or the orthodontics or that drunk dad who showed up at a dance to hit her across the face, or that poor creature who somebody needs to tell *You smell, fix it, or it will never, never, never get better for you*. The days were all day every day, get a grade, take a note, put something on, put somebody down, cut open a frog and see if it's like this picture of a frog cut open. But at night, the nights were you, finally on the phone with you, Ed, my happy thing, the best part. (Handler and Kalman 2011, 82)

"I am putting this in the 'life in high school' section of our library reluctantly. I almost don't want to let it go yet, but I also want you to have it. If you are interested, add it to your next list and be prepared for a fast read."

Books Turn Students into Readers

I guarantee that introducing several books a day at first will help you connect many of your students to books they want to read. You can bet that some of your students have been readers all along and will have books they're in the midst of on that first day of school. Others used to love reading and will be led back fairly easily.

Most years that leaves me with a stubborn 30 percent or so that make me work—and not just in the first few weeks. These are the kids who might start and drop a book every few days for the first quarter of the year. You'll think you've finally met that kid that will never be a reader. You'll feel like you've done all you can. You might even listen to a colleague who says some kids just don't like reading. Don't listen; don't you believe it. Reading is oxygen for a student's future success. There is no giving up here. Every kid. Every year. As Nancie Atwell (2007) says, "For students of every ability and background, it is the simple miraculous act of reading a good book that turns them into readers. The job of adults who care about reading is to move heaven and earth to put that book into a child's hands" (28).

Tyler was one of those readers. He never got beyond a hundred pages in any book I recommended for almost an entire semester last year. I'll never forget his thrill at finding the right book. He bounced into my room that morning and said, "Mrs. Kittle! I read the whole thing!" I joined his celebration. Tyler went on to read three more books by January and left a letter on chart paper for my next semester's students. He told them to find a book soon because there were so many good ones they might never know otherwise. He told them that he couldn't believe all the good books he'd missed in all of his school years, and he left his email address for anyone who wanted recommendations from him while he was off in training for the Coast Guard after graduation. Tyler is one story of many but too important to ignore. The book that finally captured him was the story of a famous baseball player's drug use and eventual recovery. He wanted to know, so he wanted to read. The book did the work that I couldn't do. Books are co-teachers in our drive to get kids reading.

One thing I love about book talks is that I can share my passion—show my students why I love literature and why they must read a book I loved—but I don't have to sell *every* student *every* day. All students become better readers and many who came in as accomplished skimmers want to go back and see what they missed in *The Adventures of Huckleberry Finn* or *As I Lay Dying*.

I once heard that a key difference between readers and nonreaders is readers have plans. A to-read-next list helps when students come to class having just finished an engaging book and are reluctant to start another. A list they created will lead them more quickly to that next book, especially if I'm conferring with another reader that morning. I am always teaching and organizing toward independence for students and the to-read-next list is critical.

How do we get students to challenge themselves in reading? I wonder sometimes if we treat reading and all things school—if we treat *learning*—like something so unpleasant and unnatural as to require dog biscuits to get them to do what we want. "You want a treat? A little extra credit?" I hear a teacher's voice pleading over the students' resistance to reading a book she has chosen. But you don't have to bribe kids to challenge themselves in reading. I'll just say, "This book, *Little Bee*, by Christopher Cleave, is a reach book. Because of its length. Because of the dual narrators you need to keep in your head and tune your ear to hear. Because of the setting—Nigeria and England—that you won't recognize. And because the payoff you feel yourself waiting for—the understanding you want—comes late in the story. There is plenty to interest you along the way, don't get me wrong, but this book requires attention and stamina and you may not be ready for it yet," and some of my strongest readers will put it on their to-read-next list. Especially once I read the voice of Little Bee, who narrates half the novel:

> I am only alive at all because I learned the Queen's English. Maybe you are thinking, that isn't so hard. After all, English is the official language of my country, Nigeria. Yes, but the trouble is that back home we speak it so much better than you. To talk the Queen's English, I had to forget all the best tricks of my mother tongue. For example, the Queen could never say, *There was plenty wahala, that girl done use her bottom power to engage my number one son and anyone could see she would end in the bad bush.* Instead the Queen must say, *My late daughter-in-law used her feminine charms to become engaged to my heir, and one might have foreseen that it wouldn't end well.* It is all a little sad, don't you think? Learning the Queen's English is like scrubbing off the bright red varnish from your toenails, the morning after a dance. It takes a long time and there is always a little bit left at the end, a stain of red along the growing edges to remind you of the good time you had. So, you can see that learning came slowly to me. On the other hand, I had plenty of time. I learned your language in an immigration detention center, in Essex, in the southeastern part of the United Kingdom. Two years, they locked me in there. Time was all I had. (Cleave 2010, 2–3)

Book talks rest on my belief that reading is not about coercion but promise. We don't have to offer rewards, we need to show students why the books deserve their attention. Then we get out of the way and let the books do the work.

Book Talk + Text Study = Using a Book Talk to Teach the Qualities of Writing

Teachers are pressed for time. I need to introduce a book that might charm a few readers into engagement, but I also have to teach students how narrative voice is built through language. I copy pages 6 and 7 of *Winter's Bone*, by Daniel Woodrell, for the class. Each student needs a copy to mark up with *noticings*—annotations of word choice, details they see, feel, smell, taste, know to be true. We are going to analyze a writer's craft as I introduce a book.

Curriculum that makes sense is important, so I don't study *Winter's Bone* when we're in the midst of writing argument. The descriptive, vivid writing that I want students to pay attention to in this text is married to a voice that creates character. Those are story skills. My text study of *Winter's Bone* occurs during our narrative unit.

I read the passage aloud and ask students to underline lines they like and phrases they think are well written; in other words, to notice what is happening in the craft of this text. Remember that reading aloud is a most important foundation in teaching writing. Paying attention to the craft of poetry is a frequent activity in my classroom, so students develop an understanding of annotation throughout the year.

I ask students three questions while I read:

1. (*At the end of the first paragraph*) What do you think is wrong with Mom?
2. (*Checking on students' ability to use context clues to determine the meaning of unfamiliar words*) What do you think *comely* means?
3. (*After the dialogue on page 7, to connect the elements of argument and narrative*) How would you describe the economic condition of this family based on evidence in the text? (*I want students to understand that the qualities of writing in any genre are similar. Details in a story are evidence for ideas.*)

I continue reading aloud through the next paragraph so my students don't miss this original and vivid simile:

> Sonny and Harold were eighteen months apart in age. They nearly always went about shoulder to shoulder, running side by side and turning this way or veering that way at the same instant, without a word, moving about in a spooky, instinctive tandem, like scampering quotation marks. (Woodrell 2007, 7)

I collect these annotations at the end of class as an exit slip (Daniels, Zemelman, and Steineke 2007) and quickly skim them while on hall duty. This is not graded work, although it can be. I use it to survey students' proficient-reader skills (as identified by Zimmermann and Hutchins 2003). I learn that most of my students are proficient readers (see Figure 5.1), but a few don't seem to be. Only a quarter of the students are familiar with using textual evidence to support a position. Most responses are like Isaiah's (see Figure 5.2); although he answers my question, he does not support his answers with details in the text. In my next reading conference with Isaiah I can determine whether he has a shallow understanding of skills or was just careless in his annotations. (Which would you conclude based on his answers?)

Figure 5.1 Winter's Bone *Pages*

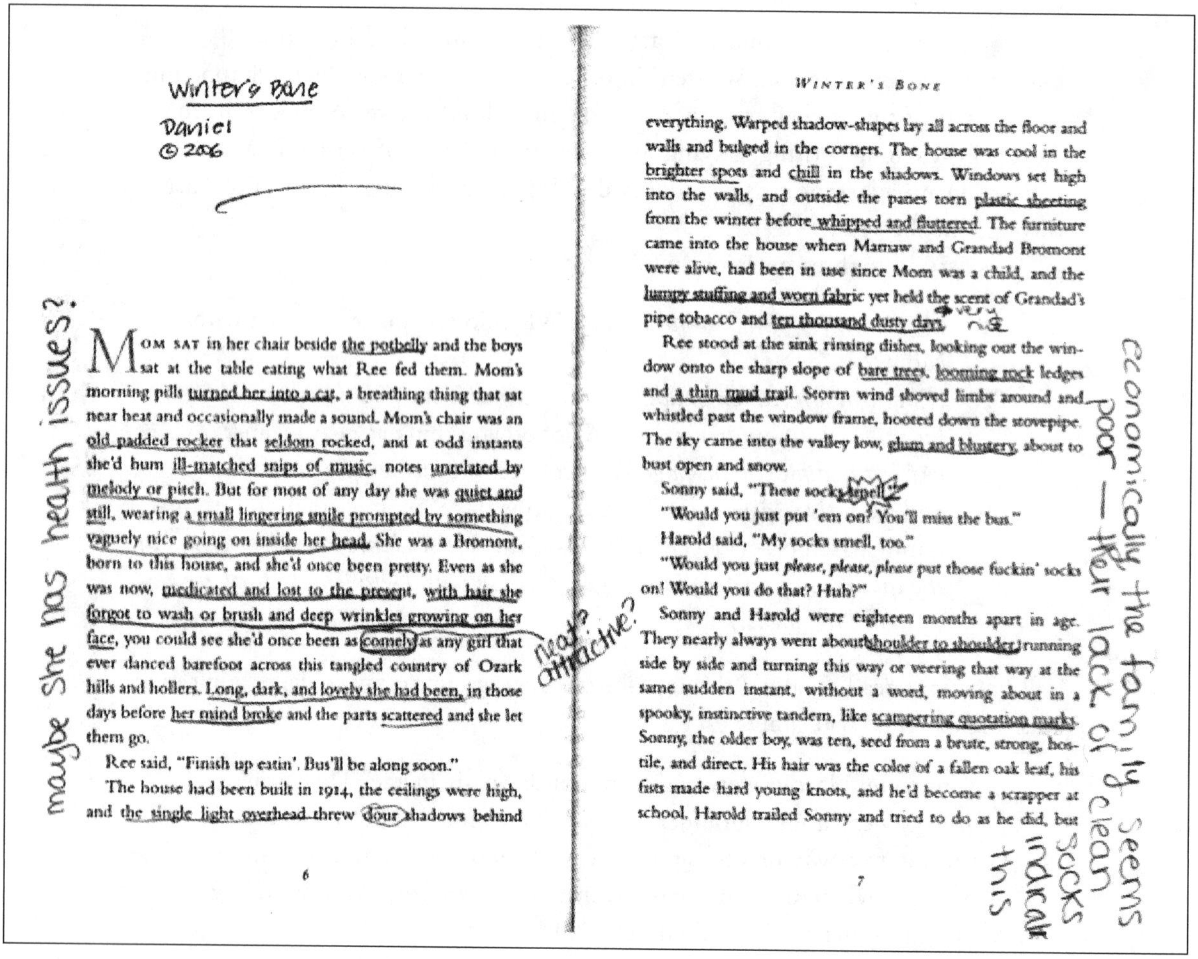

Winter's Bone
Daniel
© 2006

maybe she has health issues?

Mom sat in her chair beside the potbelly and the boys sat at the table eating what Ree fed them. Mom's morning pills turned her into a cat, a breathing thing that sat near heat and occasionally made a sound. Mom's chair was an old padded rocker that seldom rocked, and at odd instants she'd hum ill-matched snips of music, notes unrelated by melody or pitch. But for most of any day she was quiet and still, wearing a small lingering smile prompted by something vaguely nice going on inside her head. She was a Bromont, born to this house, and she'd once been pretty. Even as she was now, medicated and lost to the present, with hair she forgot to wash or brush and deep wrinkles growing on her face, you could see she'd once been as comely as any girl that ever danced barefoot across this tangled country of Ozark hills and hollers. Long, dark, and lovely she had been, in those days before her mind broke and the parts scattered and she let them go.

neat? attractive?

Ree said, "Finish up eatin'. Bus'll be along soon."

The house had been built in 1914, the ceilings were high, and the single light overhead threw dour shadows behind

6

WINTER'S BONE

everything. Warped shadow-shapes lay all across the floor and walls and bulged in the corners. The house was cool in the brighter spots and chill in the shadows. Windows set high into the walls, and outside the panes torn plastic sheeting from the winter before whipped and fluttered. The furniture came into the house when Mamaw and Grandad Bromont were alive, had been in use since Mom was a child, and the lumpy stuffing and worn fabric yet held the scent of Grandad's pipe tobacco and ten thousand dusty days.

Ree stood at the sink rinsing dishes, looking out the window onto the sharp slope of bare trees, looming rock ledges and a thin mud trail. Storm wind shoved limbs around and whistled past the window frame, hooted down the stovepipe. The sky came into the valley low, glum and blustery, about to bust open and snow.

Sonny said, "These socks smell."

"Would you just put 'em on? You'll miss the bus."

Harold said, "My socks smell, too."

"Would you just *please, please, please* put those fuckin' socks on! Would you do that? Huh?"

Sonny and Harold were eighteen months apart in age. They nearly always went about shoulder to shoulder, running side by side and turning this way or veering that way at the same sudden instant, without a word, moving about in a spooky, instinctive tandem, like scampering quotation marks. Sonny, the older boy, was ten, seed from a brute, strong, hostile, and direct. His hair was the color of a fallen oak leaf, his fists made hard young knots, and he'd become a scrapper at school. Harold trailed Sonny and tried to do as he did, but

economically the family seems poor — their lack of clean socks indicate this

7

The next day I ask a textual-evidence question about a different mentor text, using a strong student response (including clear evidence) from our work today as a model. This allows students to *imitate* using specific evidence to support thinking and builds a foundation for being able to use the skill independently.

One benefit of short passage study during book talks is engagement. If I choose a truly terrific passage, many students become interested in the book. It ends up on more to-read-next lists than if I simply summarize and read a bit as usual. It also allows me to show the great writing I want students to study in a book like Booker Prize–winner *Wolf Hall*, by Hilary Mantel (a book most students won't choose, because it's long and set in sixteenth-century England). Short texts help create a bridge that leads more students to attempt a longer, more difficult text.

Figure 5.2 Winter's Bone *Pages*

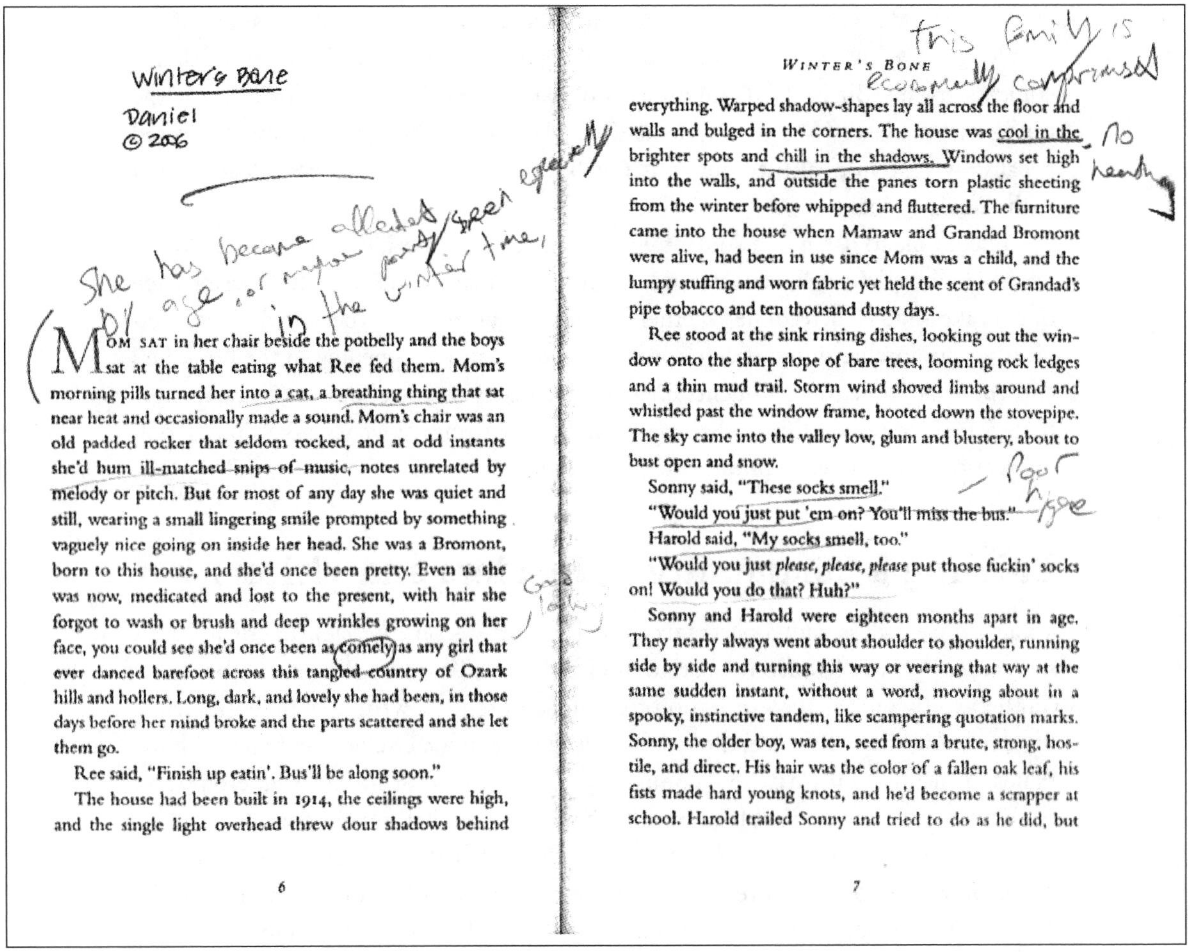

MOM SAT in her chair beside the potbelly and the boys sat at the table eating what Ree fed them. Mom's morning pills turned her into a cat, a breathing thing that sat near heat and occasionally made a sound. Mom's chair was an old padded rocker that seldom rocked, and at odd instants she'd hum ill-matched snips of music, notes unrelated by melody or pitch. But for most of any day she was quiet and still, wearing a small lingering smile prompted by something vaguely nice going on inside her head. She was a Bromont, born to this house, and she'd once been pretty. Even as she was now, medicated and lost to the present, with hair she forgot to wash or brush and deep wrinkles growing on her face, you could see she'd once been as comely as any girl that ever danced barefoot across this tangled country of Ozark hills and hollers. Long, dark, and lovely she had been, in those days before her mind broke and the parts scattered and she let them go.

Ree said, "Finish up eatin'. Bus'll be along soon."

The house had been built in 1914, the ceilings were high, and the single light overhead threw dour shadows behind

6

WINTER'S BONE

everything. Warped shadow-shapes lay all across the floor and walls and bulged in the corners. The house was cool in the brighter spots and chill in the shadows. Windows set high into the walls, and outside the panes torn plastic sheeting from the winter before whipped and fluttered. The furniture came into the house when Mamaw and Grandad Bromont were alive, had been in use since Mom was a child, and the lumpy stuffing and worn fabric yet held the scent of Grandad's pipe tobacco and ten thousand dusty days.

Ree stood at the sink rinsing dishes, looking out the window onto the sharp slope of bare trees, looming rock ledges and a thin mud trail. Storm wind shoved limbs around and whistled past the window frame, hooted down the stovepipe. The sky came into the valley low, glum and blustery, about to bust open and snow.

Sonny said, "These socks smell."

"Would you just put 'em on? You'll miss the bus."

Harold said, "My socks smell, too."

"Would you just *please, please, please* put those fuckin' socks on! Would you do that? Huh?"

Sonny and Harold were eighteen months apart in age. They nearly always went about shoulder to shoulder, running side by side and turning this way or veering that way at the same sudden instant, without a word, moving about in a spooky, instinctive tandem, like scampering quotation marks. Sonny, the older boy, was ten, seed from a brute, strong, hostile, and direct. His hair was the color of a fallen oak leaf, his fists made hard young knots, and he'd become a scrapper at school. Harold trailed Sonny and tried to do as he did, but

7

Reading, Reading, Reading

Students read in my class for three critical reasons. First, I need to *see* their engagement with their books (which I can tell in a quick look around). Second, while the students are reading, I have time to confer. Third, students need to practice this central skill.

Last month I sat in our ninth-grade team meeting as the teachers discussed a novel unit. The advanced students were assigned *To Kill a Mockingbird*, and the teacher planning the study asked, "Did you give them time to read in class last year?" The team leader said, "Honors? Of course not."

I have a problem with this. It makes no sense. We give students time to work on projects. We give them time to watch two-hour videos of the books we teach. We give them time to sit and listen to other students discuss a book they didn't read the night before. We consider those valid uses of time, but not reading. Why not?

New standards require new lessons, but we feel we can't let go of some of the past lessons we know are valuable, so we squeeze more into each hour and rush our students from 7:30 to 2:30. Administrators shave another minute or two off the time between classes. We give students too little time to write about content covered because we are in a rush to cover as much as possible. Of course we lose in that rush. Our students lose.

I take time to listen to a student who in week 7 of the semester still hasn't found a book he loves. I might recommend seven or eight titles and quickly describe each one. I take time to determine whether a student who receives special education services for comprehension difficulties understands what is happening in the book he's chosen. I take time to let students uncover what they notice about craft in a mentor text instead of telling them what makes it good writing. Voyages take time. Good instruction takes time. Creating readers takes time.

Building a Community of Readers and Writers

Today I started class with a book talk (of course). It was on *Encyclopedia of an Ordinary Life*, by Amy Krouse Rosenthal, and I also used a passage from the book for our text study plus as the inspiration for guided notebook writing: a potential triple play, you might say. By the end of class I felt like a winner, circling the bases with my hands in the air. Our classroom community rallied on an ordinary Wednesday, and the energy and laughter bubbled into the hall when the bell rang. Score.

I want to be sure you realize how rare this is before I say any more about it. Triple plays are not made every day. In the entire history of recorded baseball trivia, 1876–2011 (Society for American Baseball Research), there were only 689 triple plays. There were just 35 in the last decade. Unlikely. Inspiring. Surprising. I want students to find those things in my classroom. There is energy in surprise.

There are dozens of well-crafted books. They could *all* be text studies. I could write from every one. Even though I'm tempted to plan a triple play more often, I don't. I am seduced by possibility because good writing gives me energy to write. But can you imagine how dull and lifeless this repetition would become?

"What's happening in class today, Skittles?"

"I'm going to tell you about a book, then we're going to annotate a passage, then we'll write about it."

Yawn.

Encyclopedia of an Ordinary Life is an unusual book, worthy of this triple play. If you don't know this book, you're in for a treat. I've given it as a present to many writer friends; it's that good. It is quirky and interesting because the author names things I've always been thinking but haven't paid attention to in the way she has.

I read her entries while scribbling along in my notebook, creating categories for my own life encyclopedia, then reading some more. I was a most distracted reader. I drove through town creating an encyclopedia for my car (best upgrade: heated steering wheel). Everything in my life became an exercise in creating and detailing categories. I dare you to read the book and not end up in your own notebook.

I began the class by looking at two of Rosenthal's categories: *thankful* and *3841 Bordeaux*. Here are a few things she wrote about each:

Thankful

I'm thankful for my health, my childhood, and spell-check. . . . I'm thankful my job doesn't require wearing panty hose, or a honking red nose. I'm thankful that I have not had to fight in a war. For platform shoes. For coincidences. . . . That I don't know everything that people say behind my back. . . . That I am not a Kennedy. That Hitler wasn't a twin. . . . I'm thankful for the sun—it just keeps rising, and never asks for anything in return. (195)

3841 Bordeaux

3841 Bordeaux was my address for a very long time. Technically, I lived there eleven years—from the age of three to the age of fourteen—but it felt like a hundred and eleven years. . . . 3841 felt as forever to me then as the finiteness of life feels to me now. One could count on things. Always: curled up worms on the sidewalk after it rained. Always: the comforting weekend sound of the Cubs game or the Bears game on TV; the rise and fall of the announcer's voice; the muffled roar of the crowd; not understanding any of it; steady, likeable background noise. Always: my dad's bottom drawer of neatly folded white undershirts; being able to take them to sleep in, so soft. (196)

Why did we look at two passages instead of one? Because at the center of my notebook invitations is a belief in wide-open possibilities that can lead individual writers to find something they have to say to the world. If we want good writing, we don't start with one prompt, we give writers many ways in. I not only read several of Rosenthal's compact entries during the book talk but also told students they were welcome to create their own categories, as I had in my notebook at home, and then write from their own ideas.

There was a small problem with this.

I write what I ask my students to write, sometimes before I come to class, and in this case, I couldn't share. My categories were remarkably inappropriate for modeling. Those moments when teaching are hard and I feel incapable often find an uncensored voice in my notebook.

Even without my models, students responded with their ideas based on Rosenthal's leads. Shelby wrote:

Thankful

I'm thankful for books that allow me to escape, and the clouds for occasionally crying, and for legs that carry me throughout the day. I'm thankful for all the people who have left and made me strong. I'm thankful for AA and the way it saved my mom. I'm thankful for honesty. I'm grateful for the sunshine and for growth. I'm thankful for this moment and for taking each breath.

Ashley wrote:

5 Lucerne Drive

Lucerne Drive was my address since the age of just three weeks old, where there were trees scattered throughout the yard, a deck attached to the front, and a new swingset just set up. Eighteen years later, the trees are all cut down, the attached deck now turned into a screened-in porch, and the swingset has been thrown to the side and replaced with hockey nets and a basketball hoop. Laughs and smiles turn into emptiness as there is always a reason to be somewhere else: games, a friend's house, work, anywhere. But reunited in the end, 5 Lucerne Drive will always be my home.

But Kori surprised us all with her entry on hallways:

Hallways

Step out the door and hang a right. Walk as fast as you can 'til you hit the inevitable traffic jam. Navigate carefully: beware the couple holding hands ten feet in front of you, now blocking the entire hallway while moving in slow motion. Beware of lockers being opened, people cutting in front of you, roadblocks, and shoving. Get to class as soon as possible.

Rules for Hallway Etiquette

First off, do not just stand in the middle of the hallway with 20 of your closest friends talking about something stupid like that gnarly car crash you almost got into on your way to the local Dunkin' Donuts last night. All you are doing is creating a huge mess and absolutely no one is going to be able to get around you. Try your hardest to remember that there are only, I don't know, a few hundred other people just like you doing the same thing.

Do not make out with your new BF or GF, who you have been dating for six hours, up against some poor kid's locker. They sure didn't ask for real life porn, so you probably shouldn't be giving them, and everyone else, a show.

After the laughter, Matt said, "Why don't we all write about hallways?"

"Yes!" came the answer, echoing around the room, student to student. I could see my teaching leaving the infield, heading toward the rare home run.

I ignored the clock, the list of items on my agenda. I noticed the pens poised above notebooks. We wrote. Five minutes later I stopped them. We reread and revised writing for two more minutes, as always, practicing the moves of revision. Then we shared.

Here are two bits of much longer entries, Matt's first, followed by Abby's:

Hallways

So much traffic. Why? The gangsters with their pants down around their ankles (but a belt on their pants . . . why?) are doing their swag walk to wherever they are going. Not to mention the couples on each other like white on rice. Why? What are you proving? That you are in fake high school love? Thank God for Herr Weitz, who helps keep people moving. Don't forget to walk with your shoulders squared and to hold on tight to your books because you don't know who or what is going to walk into you. You got to be ready to move people out of your way. Perhaps a stiff arm swing will do it.

Hallways

Before the bell, scattered conversation. Rushing through doorways or rushing out. Empty halls echo squeaky sneakers, clicky boots, or shuffling feet. Seeing someone that's too far to say hi to. Awkwardly smiling at the floor takes place until you realize you missed your chance. Eye contact becomes weird making hands fidget and hair twirl. Papers crinkle, passes fold, even teachers don't know what to do. They too smile at the floor and reflect on their decision to remain in this place longer than they had to.

And there was more. That's the thing about energy. It can infect the room, knocking holes through the confining walls of my classroom and allowing entry to unexpected observations. We can't always see it coming, and we can't orchestrate it or we'd do it more often, but we should certainly seize it when it arrives.

A student suggested we create our own Kennett High School Encyclopedia. We commandeered one of the classroom's whiteboards. Here we were, three days before the holiday recess, and my students were excited about writing.

Figure 5.3 *Whiteboard*

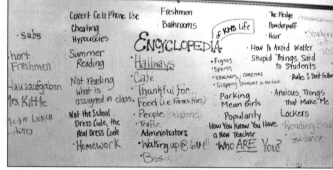

The next day the whiteboard was covered with categories (see Figure 5.3). We wrote again.

I wrote:

Prom

Okay, one time I had to police the downstairs hall at the Mt. Washington Hotel from the hideaway bar to the game room to the stairs to the gift shop, walking laps to find rebels. The only fully lit place was the game room, the one with the huge windows so you could see inside. What I saw cannot be erased from my memory. Dark-red shiny gown on the floor. White, hairy legs. Half of a tuxedo. Noises I will not repeat except for what I shouted as I covered my eyes, "Stop it! You two get your clothes on and get upstairs now."

Squeals. Giggles. Rustling fabric. "Are you kidding me?" I groaned, still blinded by my hands pressing my eyeballs into my skull.

She said, "Sorry Mrs. Kittle," in a breathless voice as she scooted out the door.

He said, "Please don't tell our dates."

Now I'm dreaming of drafting my own *Encyclopedia of a Teacher's Life,* which I realize is probably just another way to procrastinate instead of finishing this book, but there is a play with words and ideas in this project that calls to me. We all need more fun with writing. I am serious about this. Play leads to good writing, and good writing begets better writing. People will tell you there is no time for fun in today's classroom. They will say that very seriously. Don't buy it. A very busy person I know responded to my inappropriate categories with his own additions, trading colorful exclamations with me for several emails before we both went back to the serious work of teaching. I know play makes us both better teachers and better writers. His laughter is half the reason I like him, and when I hear it in his writing, I listen closely, then work to find it in my own.

I began writing my own *Encyclopedia of Writing a Book* after class that day. I am finding new entries for it all the time. Here are four:

CEREAL

First drafts reek, zap my will, and drive me to eat handfuls of Quaker Oatmeal Squares while scowling at my notebook. My Corgi waits, ears up, for the ones I'll drop.

FEAR

No one will read my book.

Worse: Those who read it will tweet pithy reviews on its awfulness that I will copy into my notebook.

Worse-er: Prim *Fox News* anchor in patent-leather pumps I envy will read excerpts in sweet, sarcastic voice and snidely observe that Penny Kittle is the exact reason we need to protect our children from misguided "teachers" through performance-based pay.

Worst: I'll be kicked out of English Teacherland for suggesting that *The Odyssey* is a colossal bore to any ninth-grade boy I would have dated in high school.

FRIENDS WHO WRITE

Every writer needs a Tom Romano. Emails contain recipes I try that night, channeling his Italian accent and lip-smacking, sauce-crafting braggadocio, plus expert advice, sympathy, jokes, one-pagers written by supersmart Miami University students, and a classic sign-off that makes me feel strong and capable: *You take care, good woman.*

WONDER

My teaching life has been built around children, teenagers, and books: those I read and those I write. Despite the political motivations that lead our schools toward mediocrity, we teachers are, as Dan Beaty would say, "still here, still alive, still teaching, with the power to change this world one little boy and girl at a time." I live in wonder.

But there is something else that happened in my students' work this day, which is a Really Big Deal: our classroom community. When Matt jumped on Kori's idea— "Let's all write about hallways!"—I saw her smile. Michael passed when it came time to share—both times—and a few students gave audible sighs of disappointment. He smiled then, too. We read, write, talk, and think together in this place. There is collaboration and interdependence in our work, and these kids belong together. *Everyone* belongs. I lamented the students absent that day. The moments that bind our students, one to another, are the very moments when we need to be most thankful. These are the moments that keep kids connected to school. Building classroom community is dropout-prevention work.

I've learned three things about building community:

- *Assign seats.* I put students into groups to mix abilities and interests. Take the time to do this. If kids always choose their seats, they choose their friends and some students are left out. Please don't let that moment happen in your room. Teenagers will avoid sitting beside students from different social groups, and they need to understand one another. Some kids can't be together, I know, but most can.

- *Change seating assignments every month.* I mix things up so that every student comes to know all of the other students during the year.

- *Build talk into everything that happens in the classroom.*
  - We read a poem a day and students often share favorite lines with someone seated nearby.

- We quick-write just about every day and then students sometimes talk about the writing in small groups. (There is always the option to pass in my room, but I pay attention when a student passes all the time.)
- We read mentor texts together and students mark up their thinking independently first, then steal the smart thinking of others at their table by talking about it (Kittle 2008).
- Students lead table talks on books they are reading.
- Students craft imitation sentences with partners.
- Students have silent conversations about a topic by writing and passing notebooks around the table.

A key component of talk for me is sharing thinking, not finding a right answer. This leads to finding authentic questions and discovering relevant answers in any writing.

The classroom community is built on moments spent writing and sharing. When I rest the writing on authentic reading it completes a cycle of engagement that sets the hook for even practiced nonreaders. I asked one boy why he stopped pretending to read in class. Even though I want to be Superteacher, creator of my own Kittle Universe of High Expectations, The One ("I would have ended up in a gutter, but I had Mrs. Kittle"), I knew his answer wasn't going to be about me. Classroom communities are essential because students care about what other students think. Listen to this boy's response:

> Because expectations were higher. Mrs. Kittle recommended good books, so I started to read them. When you see other kids around the room that haven't read since probably like first grade, and you see them enjoying a book that Mrs. Kittle recommended, then you have to kind of try reading our books. Like the book *The Hunger Games*, that book's incredible, and when you have a sequel to that and there's another book coming out in the near future, and you just want to continue reading. Once you've finished books like that, you're just like, "Dude, I *know* there are other books out there that are just as crazy as that." And then you find them and you just enjoy reading them.

Does it surprise you to know that when this boy and I met for coffee three years later we talked about books?

I've always said the books do the work to capture readers. And equal to that, the *community* of readers and writers carries the energy in the room. Over there on the sidelines, cheering them on? That's you and me.

Chapter 6

Conferences

We can likely agree that too many students are not reading enough in high school, some by choice and some because they've given up trying. I believe too many teenage readers have a fixed-performance view of their achievement, as defined by Peter Johnston (2012). He says, "The problem is that these students live in a world of permanent traits and (in)abilities. They believe that people have fixed, unchanging characteristics. They think some people are good at poetry (or math, or reading) and some are not. Some are smart, some are not, and there really isn't much they can do about it. In this world, simple events, like mistakes or unsuccessful attempts, are indicators of those fixed characteristics" (10). Contrast this with the dynamic-learning view in which people "think of ability, or intelligence, as something that grows with learning and depends on the situation. A dynamic theorist thinks that the more you learn, the smarter you get" (11). I can walk around my current classes of ninth, tenth, eleventh, and twelfth graders and find examples of each.

But here's the reason I bring it up. Johnston continues, "Children who adopt a fixed-performance frame tend to become helpless when they run into trouble. They cease being strategic—except when it comes to ego-defense" (15). This ego-defense is behind many students' refusal to read and finding ways to fake it. So many of my students have told me they just aren't good at reading, and I can hear their helplessness. That's a fixed view. Reading that is too hard for them either confirms this or convinces them they can only read well with a teacher's guidance, as dependent readers. I can lead all students through difficult texts, but unless I also manage their individual reading lives, I won't move all of my students as far as I need to. I strive to move students from a fixed-performance frame to a dynamic one through the intentional use of language that imagines they can improve regardless of their prior success. A student says, for example, "I'm not a reader." I say, "Oh, I expect you just haven't found the right book yet." This is the intentional language of conferences.

Conferences with individuals have always been crucial in my work. Don Graves first taught me to pay attention to the language of conferences while we were filming them for *Inside Writing* (2005). Don said we could determine the teaching in a workshop simply by listening to the language students use with one another. I began to listen when I observed colleagues and I began to listen to what the students in my classroom were saying. I also read *Choice Words*, by Peter Johnston (2004). Then I read it again. I bought it on CD and listened to it in my car. Johnston's research has had a permanent impact on my thinking.

To understand when and how to use language that empowers discouraged readers, you have to learn to listen well. As Johnston says, "When we are listening to a partner, we are actually doing more than that. We are offering through our bodies a responsiveness to the other that, in a sense, brings the other into being. If there is no responsiveness between us, no openness to being influenced by the other, there is no trust. It is through persistently being heard that we take ourselves seriously and view ourselves as agentive—someone who has interests and plans and acts accordingly" (102). I must take the time to hear, persistently, the struggles and plans of the individual readers in my classroom in order to know them as people and help them develop reading habits that will guide them long after they leave my classroom.

I'm afraid that using empowering language with readers might be easily dismissed these days, when Important Standards occupy all the energy in the room. But how we talk to students is larger than the standards we post in the classroom each morning. We either confirm what they believe as nonreaders or give them hope that the trajectory of their reading life can change. I'm not sure there is anything more worth getting up for each day.

Maybe all those people who control what kids read all year, who stand guard with *Antigone*, insisting that this is what we teach, just don't have the kinds of students I do. I have students who suffer when they can't do it alone. They are humiliated by dependency. I grieve for these kids. I'm not a teacher of particular standards or even of literature; I teach students. When I focus on the needs of readers, I am far more likely to help my least confident ones see a dynamic-performance frame for reading and lead them to improve their satisfaction and their skills in the time I have them. I have to convince readers they can improve because if they don't *believe* it, trying harder seems futile. Our language is a most important tool.

Two kinds of conferences occur regularly in my classroom: talk about reading and talk about writing. Both kinds teach reading *and* writing. I start these in the first week of school.

I pull my chair next to Tyronne's desk. He's a ninth grader reading *The Art of a Beautiful Game: The Thinking Fan's Tour of the NBA*, by Chris Ballard. He's about fifty pages in, but tells me he is confused. I ask him why and he starts skimming back through the chapters he's read so far, telling me he doesn't see why the author chose this or that player. I haven't read the book, but I understand quickly that what he's missing is the big picture: how individual chapters focus on a particular player or element of the game, but all chapters contribute as parts of the whole. I show him the table of contents and preview it with him, explaining how the book is organized around elements of the game. I ask him whether he has read the introduction, in which the author explains the concept of the book and its organization, and he admits he hasn't: he didn't think it was important. I skim it with him, highlighting a few things the author says—like this: "This book is about passionate players. It is not about one season or the inner workings of a team or the 'genius' of a coach, but rather about the beauty of basketball, because even the 'ugly' aspects—like, say, defense and rebounding—become beautiful in the hands of the masters" (4)—and this: "It is my hope that, in writing this book, I might inspire some of you to feel similarly: to see the game from a different perspective (or a dozen different ones), to gain a renewed appreciation for the at times misunderstood giants who roam our nation's arenas and, above all, to revel in the art of what is truly a beautiful game" (5). I ask Tyronne if he can see how the individual chapters are part of a bigger idea. He says, "Definitely. I was reading this kind of arguing with [the author] about his choices of players, but now I get these weren't his favorites, really, but the ones who did the thing best."

That conference took about three minutes. I didn't sit down expecting to talk about the table of contents or the organization of the book. I sat down to listen and learn from Tyronne's experience with reading. This conference was one of three I completed on our third day of that school year. It follows a typical architecture, a term I stole from Lucy Calkins: question and listen, recognize insights from that information, then find out whether the reader has a plan for next steps. Always, beneath it all, I try to encourage readers.

I ask a question like "How's it going?" (Anderson 2000) or "Tell me what you're thinking about your reading" or "What's this about? I haven't read it." I listen as the student talks and I think about what I can teach that will help this reader be more successful with the text or what questions I need to ask to get more information. I also think about how I can move him to believe in his own ability to improve. I try to listen more than I talk. In Tyronne's conference I centered my talk on teaching him a strategy. This day I didn't check on his to-read-next list because his question drove my conference. That's the art of responsive listening.

Reading conferences fall into three categories:

1. Monitoring the student's reading life.
2. Teaching strategic reading.
3. Helping the student plan the complexity and challenge of her reading.

My goal is to place my teaching where it can be most helpful.

It matters that I slow myself down to think about one student at a time. I consider what the student understands about his reading and push his thinking with good questions. If I want to probe into a student's comprehension, I may need more than a few minutes. I don't want to pretend that checking in ("Are you still enjoying this?") as I walk by on my way to confer with another student is at all the same as pulling my stool alongside a desk and asking, waiting, and thinking with a student about the reading. (If you're wondering how I know what was said in the conferences below, I record many conferences each year, those from my classroom as well as in rooms where I am guest-teaching, and watch and listen to them to learn from them.)

Conferences That Monitor a Reading Life

Typical questions here are:

- What are you reading? How did you choose it? How do you find good books?

- What's on your to-read-next list? Which authors are your favorites?

- How much did you read last year?

- Do you consider yourself a reader? Where do you read at home?

Lennon, a seventh grader, has *All the Broken Pieces* on his desk. I don't know this book, but I ask him where he got it. He says his teacher's book talk. I ask him what it's about and he says the Vietnam War, adding, "I'm reading it because my grandfather was in the Vietnam War." We talk about this for a moment—the importance of grandparents, the way they help us see how the world has changed.

I notice the text. "This form of poetry that tells a story—narrative poetry—is an interesting form, isn't it? Have you read anything like this before?"

He nods. "I read *Monster* last year and another one I can't remember—*Shooter*."

"Did you read a lot last year?" I ask.

He rattles off nine Matt Christopher titles, then tells me he thinks this book will be difficult. When I ask why, he tells me that the setting isn't familiar, so he thinks he'll struggle to make sense of it. Sharing a potential difficulty in his comprehension gives me my next teaching opportunity.

First, I acknowledge that anticipating challenges helps us read purposefully. I honor his reflective thinking about his reading.

Next, I explain that creating a mental image is a strategy readers use to deepen thinking. "Sketching is a great way to focus on details in setting. It can help us pay attention to details in the text we might miss otherwise. At the end of this chapter, I want you to sketch what you remember about the setting of this part of the story, going back to skim for details as you do. You will also likely imagine the setting differently than other readers do and when you share what you see, you both see more. Since Jared is also reading this book"—I nod toward a student at a different table—"I'm going to ask both of you to sketch and then compare your drawings later today. One of the great things about books is that each reader brings a unique set of experiences to reading that impacts the way we think about the book. Everyone sees a little differently." Silent reading is often followed by short discussions among readers, so the boys will have time to meet later.

What do we know? Lennon is a reader. He identifies as one and is selecting books based on his teacher's book talks and his interests, as well as challenging himself to read something he finds difficult. My goal with this student will be to continue to feed him books he's interested in, challenging him to increase the difficulty. I make a note to look for nonfiction books on the Vietnam War. I know Lennon has a reading life, so the first, most difficult hurdle is behind me. This conference has given me an opportunity to teach in response to his question and to understand him better as a reflective, purposeful reader.

It's the start of a new semester and twelfth grader Kevin arrives without a book. I ask him what he's interested in and notice his hockey jacket. He's captain of our undefeated-heading-for-a-repeat-as-state-champions team. "Have you read Theo Fluery's autobiography?" He nods. *The Boys of Winter*?"

"Yeah, twice." Uh-oh. "How about Steve Yzerman? I have a biography of him, and he is the greatest captain ever." He smiles. Most of the hockey players at my school know I'm a huge Detroit Red Wings fan. He says, "I'll look at it," and I promise to bring it to class the next day.

He hasn't read much since last summer, he tells me. "Busy," he says, as they all do. It's February. Since he didn't have English in the fall, he hasn't made time for it. I ask about his reading the year before in American Literature, and he says he read the assigned novels but hated them; *Huck Finn* was better than the rest, but *The Great Gatsby* was just horrible. I glance at his to-read-next list; it's blank. I talked about fifteen books on the first day of class, but none snagged his interest. I'm going to have to work harder.

He is headed to college but reads only what is required of him, which last year was six novels. He needs to read four times that many to develop the stamina for college reading. I believe he will: if it is expected, he'll do it. He read all the assigned work last year, but we simply don't ask enough of students. I am determined to challenge this boy as I lead him to our classroom library.

Conferences That Teach a Reading Strategy

Typical questions here are:

- How is the reading going for you?

- Is this an easy or a hard read for you? How do you know?

- Tell me about a time when this book has confused you and what you've done to get yourself back on track in your understanding.

- Tell me about these characters—who are they, what do you think of them?

- What questions are at the heart of this book? What questions might the author be trying to answer through the struggles of these characters?

- I see you're almost finished with the book. When you think back over the way a character has changed in this story, can you point to specific moments when something was revealed about this character? Could you make a claim about this character and support it with evidence from the text?

- How is this book different from the last book you read?

I kneel beside eighth grader Amaari. I am guest-teaching in a colleague's class, so I don't know him, and his body language tells me he is not interested in talking to me. I try anyway. He doesn't have a book this morning and tells me he finished *The Hunger Games* a week ago. I ask him whether he's interested in reading the next in the series, and he shrugs. "Can you tell me one thing that sticks with you from *The Hunger Games*?" I ask.

"Don't know." He looks away. "Forgot."

"Well, I thought Katniss was a pretty interesting character," I say.

"Yeah, she went in because her sister's name was drawn in the lottery, only she went instead."

I'm encouraged. He's talking. "Yeah, I remember that part," I say. "Tell me more." (If there is one enduring phrase I learned from my years with Don Graves, it's that one. He was a deep listener and often responded with a pause, then, "Tell me more.")

He looks away. "I don't remember."

"Well, were you surprised at who won in the end?"

"I don't remember." I wait. He looks at the wall.

"Do you remember Peeta?" I ask.

"No."

I wait for a response, but he doesn't want to talk to me. "So you said you weren't that interested in the next book in the series, do you have any books on your to-read-next list?" He shakes his head. "Well, I'll see whether I can find a book you might be interested in. What are some things you like to do?" He looks away while I'm talking.

He picks up a book on the table, "I'll just read this," he says and opens it, ending our conference.

What has emerged from this conference? Well, I'm pretty confident that Amaari did not read *The Hunger Games*. He may have started it, he may have read the back cover, but I can't imagine a kid can have finished the book a week ago and not remember the ending. This conference may have been unsuccessful simply because Amaari and I do not have a relationship. Knowing students is an essential first step.

As far as his life as a reader, he has no plans for reading and is not interested. What do I do with this information? It makes no sense to turn this into a confrontation; rather, it tells me I need to find a book he can and will read. I know that until we have Amaari reading, we won't see the improvement we seek. Engagement is always job one.

"What are you reading?" I ask, kneeling beside the desk of Chung-Hee, a ninth-grade English language learner at the International School Bangkok.

"I haven't read that much. I'm reading the first twenty pages."

"What is it? How did you choose it?" Although I don't know the title, Chung-Hee tells me his teacher recommended it. When I ask whether his teacher recommends good books, he says, "Yes, often." (The impact we have on readers' choices is powerful.)

"What did you read before this?"

Here he hesitates. "I was reading—uh—I forget the name of it." Finally, "I was reading *Mice and Men*." The class has just finished reading this together. and there are posters and activities displayed around the room.

"What did you think of that one?"

Again he hesitates. "It was good and maybe it was kind of new. It was to make me more—more understand stories."

"How is this book different?"

"It's kind of easier to read. It more makes sense because the characters are from Korea, and I can make more connections to my life because the character plays soccer and I play soccer." While he speaks his shoulders relax and he speaks more rapidly. The book is definitely easier in vocabulary than *Of Mice and Men*, but Chung-Hee has also identified what makes reading feel easier to a novice—making connections between his life and the characters and situations in the book. It is ideal when young readers can use what they learn in whole-class reading to help them understand their independent reading. Because he has just begun reading, I don't press him on comprehension, but this is a natural next step.

Brad, a ninth grader, is reading *Cirque du Freak*, the first in a twelve-book series, The Saga of Darren Shan. He found it in the classroom library and plans to read the entire series. In a few brief exchanges I determine that he has no trouble understanding the plot, so I ask, "How old are the boys in the story?"

"Ten to twelve."

I think it helps that I told him I don't know this series. My question sounds less like a reading quiz question, more like simple interest in the story. "Do they act like ten- to twelve-year-olds that you know?"

"Yeah," he answers quickly, laughing.

"Yeah?" I ask, waiting for more.

"There's four of them," he says, "but they could only get two tickets because they didn't have enough money, so they do rock-paper-scissors to decide who gets to go." We both laugh.

"Definitely age ten to twelve," I say.

I discover through questioning that Brad has read the Alex Rider series and is considering *The Hunger Games* trilogy because of the action, so I write *fast action/ literature?* in my notes to prompt my thinking later. Students will tire of the same thing, even if they choose it, and he will tire of these plots. I want to build a ladder of complexity (an idea well developed in Teri Lesesne's 2010 book *Reading Ladders*) of books with fast action but increasingly complex characters, vocabulary, and situations.

Conferences That Increase Complexity and Challenge

Typical questions here are:

- What else have you read by this author? What other books have you read that are as difficult as this one?

- Which books on your next list are challenging? Have you considered how to push yourself as a reader?

- Which genres have you read this year? Tell me about a genre you don't usually read and let's think about books that might ease the transition from what you love to what will challenge you to think differently.

- Tell me about a book you've dropped this year. Why did you drop it?

- How are the books you've been reading this year similar?

Tenth grader Adrienne is reading *The Hitchhiker's Guide to the Galaxy*, and I wedge myself between desks in a crowded classroom, kneeling at her level. "Tell me what you think of this," I say.

"My dad recommended it. I wanted something that no one else in this class was reading. Something different."

"And?"

"Well, I want more depth from these characters," she says. "There are a lot of characters, but each one just skims the surface."

Since I have read and enjoyed the *The Hitchkiker's Guide*, I spend a few minutes chuckling over the book with Adrienne. I tell her that I hadn't thought about the depth of the characters before, probably because the plot is such a ride, but that I like her insight. I think about books with deep explorations of character I can recommend she add to her to-read-next list.

First I suggest a book with multiple narrators, because you understand more each time another character takes over the telling of a story. She is interested in *Trash*, by Andy Mulligan, and *Extremely Loud and Incredibly Close*, by Jonathan Safron Foer. *Trash* is below her reading level but will teach her about another part of the world while introducing her to multiple narrators. I explain that Foer's book will be a reach for her—and is for most students—because it's hard to understand the way the two narrators intersect. I tell her readers can pay closer attention to the information the author is giving them and work past their confusion but that it takes stamina to continue to read and reread until it makes sense.

Adrienne responds as most strong readers do. Both titles go on her to-read-next list, and she puts a star next to Foer's book. Students want challenge. If she begins reading it, I will need to monitor her comprehension and teach into what she understands and what confuses her.

Ninth grader Park is nearly finished with *From a Buick 8*, by Stephen King. He has read eight of King's books so far and is set to read *The Tommyknockers* next. Clearly, Park has a reading life. I ask, "Tell me what you've noticed about King's writing." Students who read several books by one author begin to see the craft at work but often don't realize what they know until they begin talking. It is a great opportunity to push their understanding. Park studies me for a moment.

"He's a good writer," he says.

"And?"

"Well, he writes more than just spooky stories. That's what people think about him."

I nod. "I confess, Park, I've only read *The Stand*, so I'm no authority, although I've made that same spooky assumption, because many of his books have been turned into movies."

It isn't my imagination. Park sits up taller. There is something powerful about giving students the authority to teach us. "Stephen King writes about life. It is like life lessons, but he uses tension to get readers. So he writes about Carrie as this evil character who goes crazy at the senior prom, but that's not the story. The story is about how high school destroys character."

"And he does this in all of his books?" I press.

"All of the ones I've read."

"I think your understanding can teach me and the rest of the class more about his work. Will you lead an author talk on his work?" He smiles and I sign him up for next week. In order to prepare for this, Park will have to think more carefully about this question, analyze King's work, and then figure out how to explain that to his classmates. This is good work for him.

My work is to figure out the next step on a ladder of increased reading complexity. I want to find works of literature that have suspense and rich plots. I return the next day with Cormac McCarthy's *The Road*, Mary Shelley's *Frankenstein*, and Kazuo Ishiguro's *Never Let Me Go,* which have compelling plot lines but are also deeply complex. I set them on his desk so he can browse through them and consider whether they're a good fit.

Sam, a ninth grader, is reading *Fast Food Nation* when I sit down to talk. His teacher recommended it, and he has found it pretty interesting so far. First I ask him about the difficulty of the text, which he describes as average. He says there are a lot of words he doesn't know.

"What do you do when you don't understand a word?" I ask.

"I write it down."

"Really? That's disciplined!" I talk with him briefly about being able to determine a word's meaning by others around it, the context of the sentence, if it reappears, etc., and he nods. "Yeah, sometimes I do just figure it out later." I am encouraged that he is aware of the difficulty and is working to bridge it.

Because I know this book and have conferred with a number of students who have started reading it and dropped it, I ask him what he does when he comes to a part in a nonfiction book that he doesn't like. As examples, I mention the slaughterhouse chapter in *Fast Food Nation* and an overly technical description of equipment in a war book I read. He says he drops the book. I suggest that he can skim the uninteresting or disturbing chapter and pick up again with the next chapter. I tell him I wouldn't have finished *Fast Food Nation* if I didn't skim the part that made me queasy and that I know many other readers who do this. Sam says he'll consider it.

I end the conference by suggesting three books by Michael Pollan that offer solutions in addition to just stating a problem like *Fast Food Nation* does. I am hoping to expand Sam's thinking. Reading several authors on the same subject shows us the power of voice and structure in a text and exposes us to idiosyncratic writing styles.

The next day in class I introduce *Can't Buy Me Love*, a biography of the Beatles, and Sam tells me he'd like to check it out and begin reading it now, since he always has several books going at once. I encourage him. Readers in my classroom often juggle more than one book, because I treat them like readers. Most readers I know read more than one book at a time. He finishes both two weeks later.

I sit beside eleventh grader Adelina. She has *When I Was Puerto Rican*, by Esmeralda Santiago, open on her desk. I am guest-teaching in this classroom and notice that she is not reading one of the literature circle memoirs the other students are reading. "I'd love to talk to you about what you are reading," I say.

She tells me she has finished *A Hole in My Life*, by Jack Gantos, and has returned to the book she was enjoying before her class began reading in small groups. When I ask why she likes it, she says it is the back-and-forth between Spanish and English. She misses home, she tells me, and this book takes her back.

I ask if she can show me a place in the text where this back-and-forth happens. She turns to the opening and shows me a poem, then its translation. I ask, "Is this a good translation?" and she says, "Not at all." She sees my surprise and explains that the words do not hold the richness of the images in the Spanish language. She also says that when Santiago wants to explain something, she uses Spanish adjectives in the midst of the English translation, and it helps her see and remember her home in a way that the English words do not.

I tell her it that she's probably gotten a lot more out of the text than I would have, since I don't speak Spanish. She nods. I then ask, "Have you thought about using some Spanish words in your memoir?" To me this is a simple leap, from what she's reading to what she's writing, but I see Adelina hasn't made it. I continue, "Think about writing like this—where you could have some of the things in Spanish, like adjectives and things?"

She says, "I never think about it," but she smiles.

I persist. "Wouldn't that be kind of cool to bring that into your piece?"

She smiles again. "Yeah, it would be cool, but I never think of it—"

"You know what I think you'd have to do? At the end you'd have to have like a glossary—'this is what this means'—unless your teacher speaks Spanish, which I don't know if she does." I stopped here to give Adelina an opening to respond, but it struck me as I was saying "your teacher" that if the teacher is the only audience for a piece, students make decisions based on that. I wish I had talked to Adelina about all the possible audiences for her piece—thought bigger about the vision of her writing—in that moment of our conference. I wish schools were places where we all thought about audiences beyond teachers, thought about writing beyond assignments, but I'm afraid we don't always. We have to connect students with many readers, especially with the myriad of ways to publish online. When we write for others, we write better.

At the end of the conference Adelina's teacher refers her to other memoirs that blend languages, and Adelina shares that she won a prize for writing in her village in Spain and loves to write. I ask her if she'll email me her memoir when she finishes it.

This conference unfolds the way it does because of what my students have taught me about building their individual reading lives. They read differently because they are reading what is personally meaningful. Many students come to see the books they read as mentor texts. I believe this leap in thinking is a result of a combination of two factors in my classroom: regularly analyzing short mentor texts as we seek vision for our writing, and reading independently throughout the school year. The more students read, the more they can see in their reading.

Conference Records

I keep a pad of paper on my clipboard with a page for each student, and I cycle through the pages, day after day, class after class. If a student is absent, I write *absent* in my conference notes and move on. I have had classes of thirty-four, requiring more than two weeks of constant work to talk to every student. During the gap between conferences many students will finish one book and start the next. I can't talk to every student about every book she reads. As Kelly Gallagher has said, students need to read four times what we can assess to improve enough as readers in the time we have them. Conferring is vital, but it isn't my only indicator of engagement. Scanning the room I can tell in a moment which students are reading and which are faking it. In addition, students talk about books all the time in my class, mostly with each other, and eavesdropping gives me lots of information.

I would like more time with each student, but I work with what I have. Daily reading conferences are three or four minutes long. I listen well and take notes.

However, I also chat with students as I stand in the hall before class or when I notice a student considering choices in our classroom library or when I check in with a kid who I know needs more frequent support. I don't record these moments, but students know I'm always thinking about them as readers and checking to see that they've found a book that's a good fit. There is an essential "with-it-ness" about engaged teachers: we watch, pay attention, respond to students, and seek the spark that says students are thinking. They know what we care about.

One morning just as I closed the door Clancy threw it open and reached in just far enough to grab my arm, "Mrs. Kittle," she shrieked, "you have to come out here and talk to me about *Nineteen Minutes*." She didn't want to ruin the ending for anyone in class who might decide to read it, but she had to talk about it. So of course I did. Conferences are obviously far superior to a quiz. Listening, probing, and responding to a student's thinking is at the heart of the conference, and it tells me not only what is understood but how the student makes sense of the text. The few minutes Clancy and I spent in the hall told me about her understanding of the whole book as she processed the author's choice regarding the ending. Don't be seduced by online reading quizzes that reduce thinking to recall questions. Readers do not grow under those conditions.

Reading conferences give me an opportunity to model strategies a student needs to use independently. I have heard myself say, "You and I will try to figure this out," and I know I'm teaching a process for reading, a strategy for making sense by rereading, that a student might not learn otherwise. Richard Allington (2001) found that "even small increases in the amount of daily teacher demonstration produced improved reading achievement" (31). And when you consider that these short, whispered conferences are done within earshot of several students nearby, they also teach others.

If we could manage it, we'd confer with individual students about their reading every day. Imagine all we could learn and all we could teach. But you might also be imagining a roomful of students wasting time while waiting for you to approach them. You could be right. I watched silent reading in a tenth-grade class fall apart one afternoon. After just two minutes, more than half the students were beginning whispered conversations and passing notes to each other. The teacher frowned at me and said, "See? Silent reading doesn't work with these kids."

But the problem wasn't silent reading. When class ended, I asked one of the boys, "How come you weren't reading when your teacher gave you time to read?"

He said, "I hate *Huckleberry Finn*. I'm not reading it." He had the shortcuts down, so being given time to read in class was time he could waste.

During silent reading in my class, the students I'm not conferring with have all chosen books uniquely matched to their ability and interests, so they are almost always reading intently. They are engaged in the most important work we know of to improve independence in reading: they are practicing reading. The importance of this time cannot be overstated. The decline in students' reading outside school requires that we allow time for reading during school (Kaiser Foundation 2010).

Conferring with readers allows me to get to what's important. I ask ninth grader Gwyneth what she's thinking about *Catching Fire*, and she says she is thinking about how the government is using the players and doesn't care about Katniss and Peeta at all. I ask, "How do you know this?" (I often follow up a student's observation or claim about the text with a request for evidence.)

She says she thinks that all governments only care about power, not people. I press her. "But where in *Catching Fire* did you see this?" Since the question stems from Gwyneth's observations, it doesn't feel like a test. It takes her a minute or more of silent skimming to find the place, and I wait.

Our conference is just a moment in a busy school day, but it feels just right: two people talking about the big ideas in books and how they make us think more deeply about life. As Suzanne Collins says, "I wish I could freeze this moment, right here, right now and live in it forever" (2009, 245). I make it happen regularly enough in conferences to remind students that their thinking is at the heart of what's important in reading.

Faith, Hope, and Love, These Three

~*~*~

In the rock-paper-scissors of life, love is rock.

—Sara Zarr

Faith has kept me teaching for almost thirty years. There's faith in kids because I know they will delight and amaze me each year. I'm naïve and gullible, it's true, but my faith in kids is never something I apologize for. There's faith in many of my colleagues and my school and what it means to be a teacher. And then there's faith in myself. That last one is the hardest—believing I'll know the right thing to say or do when I need to. Taking that risk each year keeps me on edge, though, and I like it.

Faith in books comes from the many powerful experiences I've had with them, both as a reader and as a teacher. Just when I think there isn't another book out there that will know my heart like the last one did, I find it. I step back and wonder about the experiences students are having in my room each year and confront a most important question: is reading in my classroom developing faith in books? Faith that books can match who students are and what they are seeking?

I think of three advanced students in first block last year: Nick, Jacob, and Dalton. They were all heading to engineering schools, and they were marking time in English class. They were like me when I'm asked to do something I don't want to do. Just the idea that I'm *supposed to* makes me surly.

Nick, Jacob, and Dalton were surly, that's for sure. There was no whole in the books they talked about reading, only parts. And in fact, once they confessed they only knew SparkNotes parts, the worst kind—SparkNotes can't convince anyone to value reading. It was trash to be kicked aside as they sprinted to calculus class. They not only didn't believe books mattered, they dared me to convince them otherwise. I had no faith—not against resistance like that. Throughout that long fall, Nick sneered at my suggestions and read reluctantly, rarely beating his reading rate. Jacob kept insisting, "I will not be one of your success stories." Dalton read so much I couldn't keep up, an average of three hundred pages a week through first semester. What I didn't see coming—what I'd forgotten can happen—is Dalton got the other two reading. He handed off books he loved: *Unbroken*, *Born to Run*, and *50/50: Secrets I Learned Running 50 Marathons in 50 Days*. The boys were all track devotees, among the hundred or so students who chase after a gifted coach at our high school. If reading could help them run better, they were in. By March Nick was beating his reading goal each week and Jacob had chosen *Crime and Punishment* for independent reading. I keep forgetting that the only faith I need is in books.

Hope matters, too, of course. When I take the risk to open a new book, I am hoping it might be as good as the last one I closed so reluctantly. I have students who are dead to hope.

Adam, in my ninth-grade class this year, doesn't even want to talk to me about books. We went to the library on Monday and I walked the stacks with him. His bored eyes scanned the shelves of titles; his to-read-next list remained blank. I kept after him. "Imagine the book that you would read: what would it be about?"

He took a minute to think. "I don't think there's even one out there like this, but this is what it would be: it would have a snowmobile and parts and it would be about building the ultimate snowmobile."

The librarian and I did a search for snowmobile books. Nothing.

"See?" he said.

"Do you want to know how they work?" I asked.

"Yeah. I'm interested in engines."

Perfect. One of my favorite colleagues is our auto technology teacher. He is the master of all things mechanical and he is a reader. He's saved me with more than one student. When the rest of the class went to lunch, I took Adam down to Jim's room. Jim reached out to shake his hand, and Adam stood taller, that's for sure. When Jim told him about a series of books that are funny and about building cars, Adam's eyes sparkled. That sparkle was hope. Adam knew he had to read—but now he imagined it might not be torture.

Jim took him through a worn textbook about cars that he pulled off a shelf, something to read while we try to find the other books. He showed Adam where he might start reading, warned him it was pretty dry stuff, but said it would teach him about brakes and engines. That enormous book was open on Adam's desk during silent reading yesterday.

Even I have hope now.

Yes, faith and hope matter to readers, but the greatest of these is still love.

It's hard to write about love. There are a lot of cynics out there. They'll tell you love is lots of things love isn't. Not just book love, which really makes the cynics snicker, but any love. You cannot manufacture love. Love is something that does not respond to "must," or force, but love is deeply rich, hopeful, and lasting. We leap—we follow—we rest in its peace. When we know love, it owns us. I believe once we love books, it lasts. And once we know love, we pass it on.

Taylor, a student I had as a senior last year, told me she skim-read all the things assigned her. She said, "It's easy, but I just don't like it." I want every student to sit with a book and expect good things, yet Taylor didn't believe it was possible. She was going to miss more than she knew. As Nancie Atwell (2009) said, "It is the lifelong reader who is going to find his or her way to good literature. Frequent, voluminous reading builds fluency, stamina, vocabulary, confidence, tastes and preferences, loyalty to authors, and even that cultural knowledge that Diane Ravitch advocates. Students leave our tiny school in rural Maine as skilled, literary readers. They also leave smarter about words, ideas, history, people, places they've encountered only in the pages of the rich stories they have read."

Taylor began by reading young adult literature, particularly the novels of Laurie Halse Anderson. She moved toward a complex reading life once she read *The White Tiger*, a Booker Prize winner that stretched her. She walked into my room the following Monday and said, "Mrs. Kittle, I need more books like this one." She chose *Columbine*, by Dave Cullen, and *Say You're One of Them*, by Uwem Akpan, and *Lolita*, by Vladimir Nabokov, and *Slumdog Millionaire*, by Vikas Swarup, before we parted that June. She read twenty-four books her senior year. She not only grew to love reading, she owned the distinction between skim-reading to pretend an understanding and immersing herself in deep reading that leads to thinking about life and ideas. She owned it in a way many adults never have. She found books that spoke to something inside her, something that needed to be answered.

For Taylor (and too many of my students), that door into a reading life had been closed and abandoned by senior year. In our workshop she was not coerced into difficult reading; she chose it. The result? She said she read faster by the end of the year, but she also "got more out of it and enjoyed it more." That was still not enough for me. Home this week for the holiday break, she told me she is continuing to read in her first year in college. She expects to find good books. *She seeks them.* That's what I was waiting for.

On final exams at the end of each school year I ask students to talk about their lives as readers.

Ryan said he remembers a Friday when he cut science to get to the library to finish his book. He said his mother had yelled at him the day before, "Ryan, put that book down and take out the garbage!" and then they both burst out laughing. Ryan had *never* been a reader.

Chris faked it through three years of honors classes in high school but was intrigued by *Memoirs of a Boy Soldier* when I talked about it on the first day of school. He said, "The first night of reading that book, I read a hundred pages, something unheard of in my life. I woke up at midnight that night with the light on and a book on my chest. From that point on, I made reading each night a hobby. I finished the book in three days, and from then on I was angry if I didn't have a book to read when I got home."

Habits change when students fall in love with books. Cam said, "I began reading every night before bed instead of watching television or playing video games. I would even come home from school and read before football practice. Every spare second I had I was in a book." Nik agreed, saying, "We had a goal to read at least eight books in one semester. That was kind of a shock, and I realized that I might be doing a lot of SparkNoting or lying. But then you said we had the option of reading any book we wanted with almost no exceptions. I picked up *Tuesdays with Morrie*. I made it my goal to read every night before bed, and after awhile I was reading when I got home from school. Books like this caught my attention and this is when I realized that I had finally developed a good reading habit for the first time in my life."

Liam said, "There have been many times this year when after I am settled in and ready to go to sleep, I have bounced back up, flicked on the light, and grabbed a book. Though my eyes sting from a late night of reading the next morning, I like it." Later when he analyzed his reading rate, he said, "The more you read, the better and faster you read. Going from 72 pages every two hours to 120 pages astounds me. I know I would easily be able to bust out a good 100 pages in the same-style novel that I previously recorded 72 in. I never really noticed my hastened pace, because I didn't feel like I was reading faster. I comprehend books fully, but I no longer have to read over things twice to understand."

I will be seeking that first-love experience for some of the students I'll meet this fall; they don't know yet what books can do. I'll be trying to charm others back to books that once captivated them. And I'll work to keep others burning with passion and interest—across genre, over time, from what is easy to what will compel them to struggle and grow.

But with every one of them, it is love that I'm after.

Book love is what we need.

Chapter 7

Responding to Reading

If books could have more, give more, be more, show more,
they would still need readers who bring to them sound and smell and light
and all the rest that can't be in books.

—*Gary Paulsen*

I finished Sara Zarr's *How to Save a Life* this weekend. I was physically wrapped around that story for several hours, wondering about the back-and-forth between narrators. How did Zarr create such distinctly different teenagers and then advance the plot through their eyes?

If you were my teacher and you wanted "proof" that I had read this weekend, what would that proof look like? How should we guide our students to respond to their reading, analyze the craft of writing, and anchor their reading experiences with small-group discussions? If our students *are* reading, how do we know what they understand?

The three common responses I receive from teachers are reading quizzes, class discussion, and literary-analysis essays. All are inadequate measures of individual understanding. We all know students can cheat their way around reading quizzes, and class discussion is a game for many. As Emily said, "I kinda based what I said off other people; my comments would be sorta what they said in different words." Or Alex: "You just listen to what the rest of the people in class are saying, kind of just get into the discussion by agreeing, or say, well, this really gets back to the American dream or whatever, and then you just make a bunch of stuff up." Both these honors students said they joined class discussions only to earn participation points, not because they had anything to say; both still managed As on their transcripts. Lastly, literary-analysis essays typically repeat information (already analyzed by someone else) that was discussed in class or found online.

Nevertheless, understanding is critical to reading proficiency, and analysis is an essential skill. College professors are dismayed at the decline in the ability of students to independently comprehend and analyze complex reading. My daughter was frustrated as a college freshman not only with the quantity and difficulty of the required reading at Providence College, but also because the books were most often not discussed in class. Students were expected to understand everything they read and apply that understanding to the many long papers required each semester. The professors did not review the reading or discuss the main points to check understanding. In weekly seminars led by professors, the students discussed some of the big ideas in the texts, but not all of the texts and never at the recall level. This is what we expect college to be like, but have we prepared our students for the volume and variety of genres they will encounter as freshmen?

I discussed this with Elaine Millen, Dean of Campus Development and New Initiatives for the University Systems of New Hampshire. She explained the difficulties students are having with college reading like this: "What we're seeing here . . . is that independent learning is critical. The students that come to us are reading for the sake of reading, not using the venue of reading or the skill of literacy to learn how to learn. That's been our biggest challenge. They're waiting for someone else to tell them what they need to learn rather than using the tool of reading and literacy to learn." I see this echoed in classrooms across our school. Students don't read assignments in social studies or science, because they know the teacher will go over the material in class. Elaine continued, "The increase in remedial programs is staggering; we can't keep up. Students don't know how to read to meet the objectives of the course, so they just read."

I would add, or they *don't* read. Many of my former students who failed in their first year of college admitted to not reading assigned work. And some of my former students have confessed that they completed college without doing much reading at all. Clearly, faking it can work with very bright students far longer than we would like. High school teachers do not want to be complicit in students' cheating. Yet when we require little more than recall in response to reading, students learn to bypass thinking. We want more. We want deep engagement. We want acts of careful attention. I was devoted to literature in graduate school. This love was born one rainy night on the campus of Lewis and Clark College. The early dark of January closed in around us as our professor led us through the rain and tempests in the novels of Charlotte Brontë. There was an echo between drizzle and foreshadowing, howling winds and a howling soul. Weather had been merely a backdrop as I raced along beside the heroines in *The Professor*, *Villette*, *Shirley*, and, of course, *Jane Eyre*. On this night, in the hands of a knowing guide, the weather became a force. I started leaping ahead as she spoke, skimming the pages for gathering clouds. Thinking has momentum, and discoveries compel you to seek more. In that moment I became a different reader.

I strive for that energy in my classroom. I know that when we learn to read well, we read differently. When we see and can name the gifts that authors ease into books, we uncover a blueprint in story that transfers to other reading. This new way of seeing will feed us always. But the key is *discovery*. We cannot be told. We must seek it. If I ask my students for a theme, they google it. That's the lowest level of thinking: recall. How can I set up conditions that lead them to discover?

I use writing, of course. Writing is discovery. The great surprise, as Donald Murray told me, is that when we write, we uncover what we didn't know we knew. We find new ways to see and think. It has been true in my own writing, so I believe it, but my students are harder to convince. They've written to explain their understanding of content. They've written to "prove" they've read. They've written to solve problems. They don't believe writing is thinking; they see it as performance.

My bridge between writing and thinking is notebooks. If I can get students to quick-write the first thing that comes to mind and follow that thinking, they discover the unusual, the thing they weren't thinking about, the thing that appears in their writing and must be attended to. It is voice on the page. Discovery writing uncovers the unconscious, and when a few brave students share these rough bits of their thinking, we are bound together as a community of explorers. I know there is little respect these days for writing outside the forms and purposes defined so seriously in curriculum documents, but that's where the energy lies. I make time for freewriting in notebooks because when my students understand what writing can do, they write with more attention and interest.

Students need to write about the thinking they do while reading. Nancie Atwell's unveiling of the power of literary letters in *In the Middle* (1988) and Linda Rief's *Inside the Writer's–Reader's Notebook* (2007) inform my thinking as I seek rich responses from students. I model this with my own thinking: what I don't know as I wonder and struggle and question and clarify. I answer the question, *What am I thinking about what I'm reading?* I work hard to make sense. I'm not summarizing as much as seeking understanding.

I might say, "I'd like you to consider the questions you think the author is asking in the book you're reading and what you think about these questions. Most books have questions at the center, and when we step back and think about them, we often understand more. I'm going to try this in front of you to show you what I mean. [*A copy of the flipchart I create is shown in Figure 7.1.*]

"First I'm going to tell you a little bit about the book. You probably haven't read it, so I'm going to give you the gist. I don't want you to spend a lot of time on this when you write today, so pare it down to important details." (Notice that I'm giving them a structure for the response.) I write:

I just finished reading Making Toast, by Roger Rosenblatt, which is a grandfather's story about he and his wife moving in with his son-in-law and three young grandchildren after their daughter dies without warning.

"Notice I underlined the book title. That's because I'm printing on chart paper. On the computer I would put the title in italics. I think this is enough information about the book, so I'm going to think about the questions I think Rosenblatt is trying to answer in this work." I continue composing:

I think there are lots of questions asked in the memoir. "How can a parent cope with the loss of a child?" is one. Part of the reason I wanted to read this book was to peek at a situation I hope I never

Figure 7.1 *Demonstration flipchart*

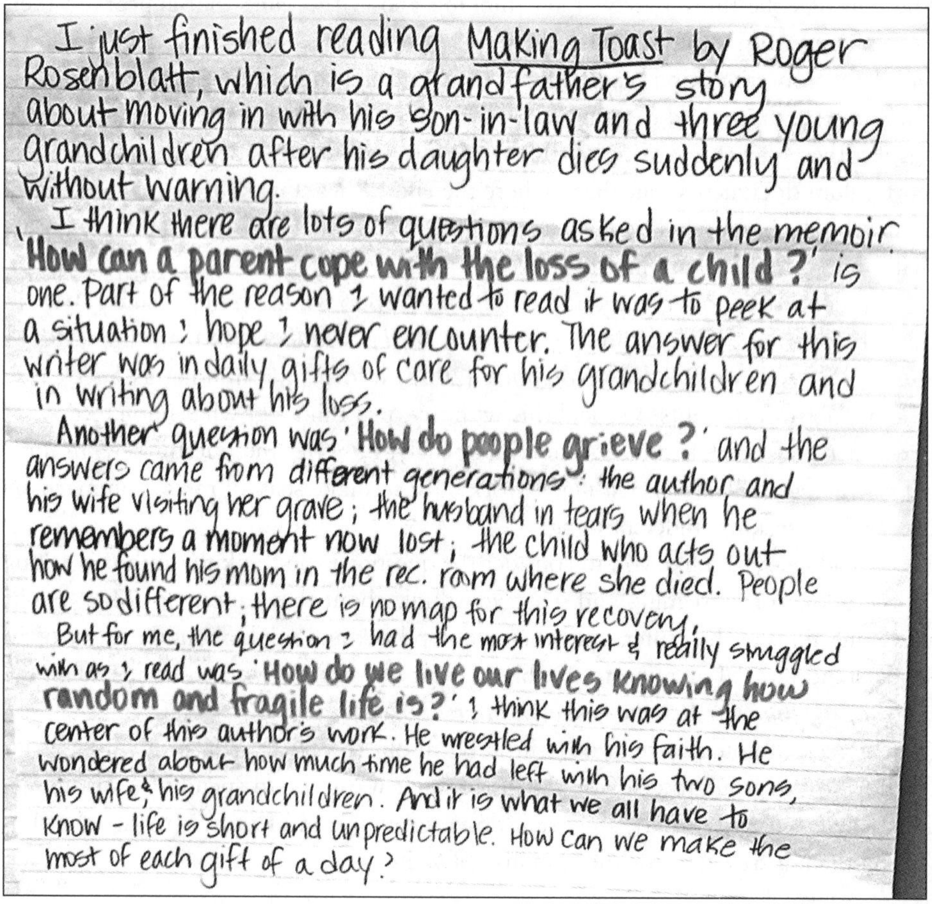

I just finished reading Making Toast by Roger Rosenblatt, which is a grandfather's story about moving in with his son-in-law and three young grandchildren after his daughter dies suddenly and without warning.

I think there are lots of questions asked in the memoir. 'How can a parent cope with the loss of a child?' is one. Part of the reason I wanted to read it was to peek at a situation I hope I never encounter. The answer for this writer was in daily gifts of care for his grandchildren and in writing about his loss.

Another question was 'How do people grieve?' and the answers came from different generations: the author and his wife visiting her grave; the husband in tears when he remembers a moment now lost; the child who acts out how he found his mom in the rec. room where she died. People are so different; there is no map for this recovery.

But for me, the question I had the most interest & really struggled with as I read was 'How do we live our lives knowing how random and fragile life is?' I think this was at the center of this author's work. He wrestled with his faith. He wondered about how much time he had left with his two sons, his wife & his grandchildren. And it is what we all have to know – life is short and unpredictable. How can we make the most of each gift of a day?

encounter. The answer for this writer was in daily gifts of care for his grandchildren, and in writing about his loss.

Another question was, "How do people grieve?" and the answers came from different generations: the author and his wife visiting their daughter's grave; the husband in tears when he remembers a moment now lost; the child who acts out how he found his mom in the rec room where she died. People are so different; there is no map for recovery.

"You know, when I started writing I had one question in mind, but as I've been writing I keep thinking of others. This is what I mean by the idea that writing is thinking. I'm thinking more because I'm writing. I've just thought of the most important question in the book, but I didn't know it until I had written the others." I return to writing:

> But for me, the question I had the most interest in and really struggled with as I read was, "How do we live our lives knowing how random and fragile life is?" I think this was at the center of this author's work. He wrestled with his faith. He wondered about how much time he had left with his two sons, his wife, and his grandchildren. And it is what we all have to know—life is short and unpredictable. How can we make the most of each gift of a day?

After this quick demonstration in which students watch me explore my thinking in writing, I have them write about their own books. Meaghan writes:

> Dear Mrs. Kittle,
>
> I am about halfway through Little Bee, by Chris Cleave. It is about a girl who escapes Nigeria to London in search of a specific family, but you don't know how she knows them. She spent two years in a detention center, and shows up on the day of the husband's funeral. The book was confusing at first because the author dodged around how the couple knew the girl. Now that he has revealed this information, it is much more clear.
>
> I can't imagine living the life that Little Bee does. It makes me think about all of the illegal immigrants that are deported each year, and I wonder if the U.S. authorities understand what they are forcing these people to return to.
>
> It is really an amazing book.
>
> *Meaghan*

Nick writes:

> Dear Mrs. Kittle,
>
> I have been working on the book <u>Unbroken</u>, by Laura Hillenbrand, for a while now. Dalton suggested it, so it must have been a good book. At this point I'm about halfway through the book and I can understand everything that is happening, but it is still slow reading. It takes me like two minutes or so per page.
>
> The book pulls the reader in emotionally, so I want to continue reading it. The book gives the reader an eye into Japanese POW camps. From this book I feel like I have witnessed some of the horrors and dangers which come with war. Being stuck out on a lifeboat for 42 days after being shot down with no food or water along with sharks, making it to land only to be captured, is just unbelievable.
>
> *Nick*

And Allie writes:

> Dear Mrs. Kittle,
>
> I am reading <u>Lolita</u>, by Vladimir Nabakov. I think everyone should read it. The story is disturbing, yes, but that is second only to its genius language. The book is so well written that I often forget that the narrator is a monster. He seems so smart and educated that you would never imagine him to do the things he has done. But his intelligence and craftiness is what allows him to control Lolita and make her believe whatever she believes.
>
> The book is personal to me because I know someone who was taken advantage of like Lolita has been. I so badly want to reach through the pages and grab Lolita and tell her to wake up!
>
> *Allie*

These notebook entries are as individual as the students who wrote them and the books they have chosen to read. They remind me that reading develops empathy. I can tell students about prisoners of war or immigration detention centers or the victims of pedophilia, and we could even skim newspaper articles on these subjects, but it would be nothing like reading deeply into an experience and understanding its complexities. Empathy is declining in our country (Kaiser Foundation 2010), and it results in the shallow rhetoric we hear on cable television. It's easy to say,

"Build a wall to keep the immigrants out," but as Meaghan found in reading *Little Bee*, we might be sending people back to horrors we can hardly imagine. Is that the right thing to do? Meaghan struggled with that question as she read. The issue's complexities challenged and engaged her and will likely have a lasting impact on her thinking.

How often should students write about reading? Every other week works for me. Asking them to write about their reading every time they read destroys the process' effectiveness. Reading students' periodic notebook entries in connection with my reading conferences allows me into students' reading experiences enough to know how to lead them to the next book that will challenge and engage them.

Students who are thinking don't need SparkNotes. Jacob explained this to me when I asked about his understanding of *Crime and Punishment* when he was about two hundred pages in. During a conference I said, "I'm curious. You say this is difficult reading. Have you used SparkNotes to help you understand it?"

He laughed. "No. Not once."

"Why not?" I pressed.

"Because you aren't testing me. If I don't understand something I just go back and reread it. I don't worry about knowing what is going to be on the test, so I'm actually able to read to just understand it."

Asking Questions That Drive Responses

There are lots of ways into thinking in writing. I ask questions all English teachers ask, reminding students to use evidence from the book to support their thinking:

FICTION

- Tell me about the narrator of your book. Is he or she believable?

- How has the author taken a flat portrait of a character and added flesh and bones? What are the moments that define a character you've connected to?

- Discuss the pace of the book. How fast or slow is the plot moving and how does that impact your enjoyment of the story?

- Trace the changes of a central character.

NONFICTION

- Does the author present enough evidence to support the main ideas of this book? Do you feel there was an attention to a variety of sources for information?

- Talk about the effectiveness of the organization of ideas in the book.

- How are the elements of story evident in this book? Would you classify the book as information/explanatory or argument?

- What are things you've learned in your reading that still have you thinking?

We keep track of questions I've asked throughout the year, so that on days we write students can use a substitute if they don't like the one I've asked. I also post the responses I've modeled. Figure 7.2 is a photo of one of my daily agendas and the sample notebook entry I wrote in front of students when they arrived.

Responding to Passages in the Book

Some days students respond to quotations from the text that they would like to say something about. I ask them to collect quotations during a few days of reading, then fill in their responses. (See the example in Figure 7.3.)

Figure 7.2 *Daily agenda/sample notebook entry*

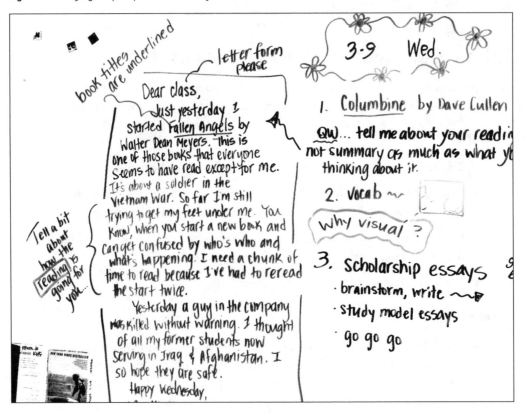

Figure 7.3 *Response to Quotations from* Reading Lolita in Tehran, *by Azar Nafisi*

Quotation/Page No.	What I Think	What This Says About the Book	What This Says About the World
"I explained that most great works of the imagination were meant to make you feel like a stranger in your own home. The best fiction always forced us to question what we took for granted. . . . I told my students I wanted them in their readings to consider in what ways these works unsettled them, made them a little uneasy, made them look around and consider the world, like Alice in Wonderland, through different eyes." (94)	I agree. I loved being transported to the world of Harry Potter. It was authentic enough to make me feel like I could be a student at Hogwarts. I wasn't interested in practicing witchcraft because of it, I just wanted to see what it might be like to walk among those that do.	Nafisi is teaching great works of literature in Iran during the years after the Shah left and Khomeni reinstituted stiff rules. She is constantly threatened with censorship. She is trying to answer the question: *Why should we read fiction?* This is why.	In many countries, the ideas in books make people afraid. It is true in America. We have battled censorship in Conway recently even. I believe that people do not read *Gatsby* and decide to be greedy or party animals or an adulterer simply because they watched him do those things in the novel. I have more respect for readers. They escape into the life of someone else and live freely in that place, but it rarely transfers to decisions they make in their lives.
"Modern fiction brings out the evil in domestic lives, ordinary relations, people like you and me—Reader! Evil in Austen, as in most great fiction, lies in the in-ability to "see" others, hence to empathize with them. What is frightening is that this blindness can exist in the best of us as well as the worst. We are all capable of becoming the blind censor, of imposing our visions and desires on others. Once evil is individualized, becoming part of everyday life, the way of resisting it also becomes individual. How does the soul survive? is the essential question. And the response is: through love and imagination." (315)	I agree that Jane Austen presents much more than you see on the surface of her work. I appreciate the depth of her characters in everyday settings. However, what I connect to most strongly about this quote is the last line. How do we survive all that we will come up against in this life? Through love and imagina-tion. A perfect answer.	Nafisi is constantly looking at what she is teaching through the lens of her personal story in Iran. I was drawn to how she joyfully continued to live in the midst of horror and constant fear. There is a section where Iraq is bombing Tehran and she wakes to hear the bombs hitting all over the city at night. She gets a blanket and goes to sleep in the hall by her kids' room. I could see myself there. Just trying to get by as insanity raged around me.	"We are all capable of becoming the blind censor, of imposing our visions and desires on others." Throughout the world peace is disturbed by the constant imposition of one will over another. It is why we have such a political divide in America right now; we refuse to see both points of view; we try to impose our vision of the world on others. No one wins.

Analyzing the Craft of Writing

My high school offers a course called Advanced Placement Language & Composition. It teaches students how to read like writers and unpack the thinking behind the construction of a variety of texts. Students who have taken this course—most don't, of course—read and write differently than those who haven't. Therefore, I use the thinking behind that class in every English class I teach. Text study anchors the work in my classroom and help writers develop a vision for their own writing (Ray 1999; Kittle 2008; Gallagher 2011). Students annotate their reading, reflecting on both content and craft as they read texts like the ones they will write. The more students understand about the craft of writing, the more deeply they can understand what they're reading independently and the more skillfully they can produce their own texts.

I begin with an example from my own writer's notebook in which I plotted the movement of the beautifully written young adult novel *If I Stay* by Gayle Forman. Here's an excerpt from the novel:

> You wouldn't expect the radio to work afterward. But it does.
>
> The car is eviscerated. The impact of a four-ton pickup truck going sixty miles an hour plowing straight into the passenger side had the force of an atom bomb. It tore off the doors, sent the front-side passenger seat through the driver's-side window. It flipped the chassis, bouncing it across the road and ripped the engine apart as if it were no stronger than a spiderweb. It tossed wheels and hubcaps deep into the forest. It ignited bits of the gas tank, so that now tiny flames lap at the wet road.
>
> And there was so much noise. A symphony of grinding, a chorus of popping, an aria of exploding, and finally, the sad clapping of hard metal cutting into soft trees. Then it went quiet, except for this: Beethoven's Cello Sonata no. 3, still playing. The car radio somehow still is attached to a battery and so Beethoven is broadcasting into the once-again tranquil February morning. (13)

I was transfixed as I walked beside this skilled writer. I read the last page of the book, then immediately began reading it again. I've only done that a few times in my life. The novel touches on a theme I had been trying to work my way through for more than a year, so it was content as well as craft that drew me in. In the weeks before I lost my father, he struggled in intensive care and we wondered if his constant pleas to "let me go" were about leaving the hospital or leaving us altogether. The character in this story is caught in the same place. My personal connection drove my initial interest in understanding how the novel was put together, but the writer in me also become fascinated, wanting to unravel Forman's craft so I could imitate it. My scene-by-scene analysis of how Forman crafted the story became more fascinating the harder I worked to make sense of it. Repeating images appeared. I saw far more than I had on my initial reading.

I knew that creating a similar storyboard could take my students more deeply into the structure of a novel, enticing them with discoveries that would lead them to analyze its craft. My students understand the concept of a storyboard because they work with one so much during our narrative units in the first few months of school. They sketch scenes and then move them around to show how their placement determines what is read and understood about their experience. (This is discussed more completely in *Write Beside Them* [2008].)

Before I present the craft analysis assignment, I first share how the richness of the book deepened as I analyzed its structure. I show students the storyboard notes I made in my writer's notebook (one page is shown in Figure 7.4). I explain that I first tried to sketch what had happened, then asked questions and looked for patterns among the scenes. I didn't know what I might find, but enjoyed the hunt.

Then I practice this concept with students by co-creating a storyboard for "The Man in the Black Suit," by Stephen King. We sketch scenes from the story and discuss character development, repeating images, and the questions at the heart of this work. We look at the construction of one scene as carefully aligned parts of a whole.

When we finish, I ask students to comb through their reading lists and select one book that they loved enough to read again. Two things are crucial in that last sentence: *rereading* and *love*. Rereading is an opportunity to see more. On the first time through a novel I am trying to figure out who is who and what is happening. I'm too engaged in understanding to analyze the book well. On a second time through, I see the whole and then the parts differently.

Jumping into analysis when students are still trying to figure out plot can be frustrating. I discovered this when I asked my UNH summer institute students (all teachers) to create a storyboard for a young adult novel as they read it. On the first morning following this homework, Toby pulled me aside. "I had trouble with the assignment last night," he told me. "The storyboarding really got in the way of my reading." I snickered. I asked him if he thought the work he assigned for students to do with their reading ever got in the way of their enjoyment. He winced. I am used to vibrant, collegial conversations in the summer courses I teach. This was different. Toby saw many nights ahead of reading and storyboarding, and he didn't like the assignment. It wasn't the amount of work I had assigned. My teacher-students needed to read the book for pleasure first, then dig into storyboarding as they *reread*. Since we only had two weeks together, I rushed it and put storyboarding into an initial

Figure 7.4 *Storyboard for the scenes in a novel*

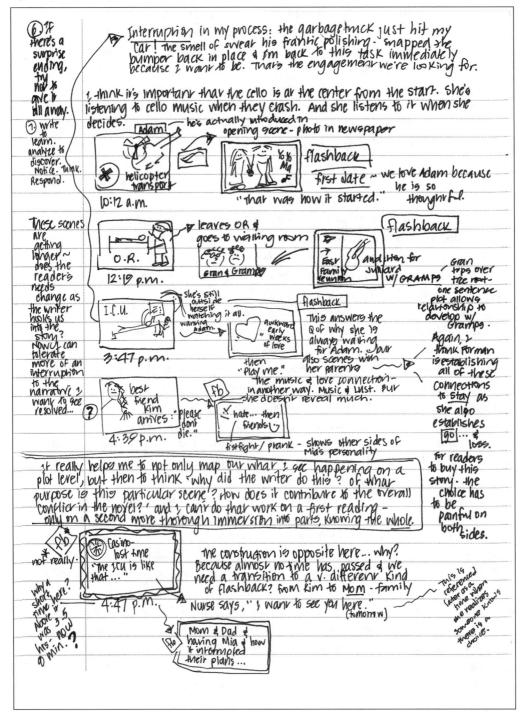

reading. It was a bad decision. Although the storyboards prompted rich small-group discussions over our time together, it was frustrating for some, instead of the treasure hunt it had been for me that summer.

My energy for learning about *If I Stay* came from my love for the book. Book choice is crucial to independent analysis. One student in my class analyzes H. P. Lovecraft's short stories to see the similarities in their construction. Two students analyze *Wintergirls*, by Laurie Halse Anderson. One boy works on Jack Kerouac's *Dharma Bums*, and eight kids gather at a back table to discuss *The Hunger Games*. Most students work alone but sit at a table with others, which prompts general small-group discussions around themes, the use of time, the development of character, and so on. Our classroom is infused with energy because students drive the questions and puzzle together over answers.

I film the vibrant group of students discussing *The Hunger Games* after watching them work for several days. This group lives collaborative thinking. They build on one another's ideas but are also quick to stand by their own ideas or demand evidence from one another to support claims made. I am fascinated by all they discover. I read a lot of young adult literature in a rush to recommend it to kids, but during this unit my students help me pay attention to how Collins uses dialogue and how scenes repeat and extend themes. I came to appreciate the craft I missed on a first reading.

We know that rereading a text is central to deepening understanding. Rereading is when we begin to think differently and see differently. There are layers of thinking that aren't accessible the first time through. As Amelia says about *The Hunger Games*, "You realized stuff you didn't realize while you were reading. When you analyze it you go deeper and deeper. Doing it made me rethink the whole meaning of the story." We want this deep rereading, because authentic, natural analysis is at the center of the work.

I stay to the side as coach and watch my students work. At times, this frustrates them. Amelia says: "I remember I'd ask you questions [about elements of the book], and I wanted your answer. Well, I didn't know I wanted your answer, I wanted *an* answer, but subconsciously I wanted *your* answer so that it would be easier. And you didn't give it to me, which was really a pain in the butt. And then I figured it out as I kept thinking about it, and I got my own answer to my own questions. I'd say as people ask you questions, don't give them your answer, let them find out their own answer."

"Why did this matter?" I ask.

"Because it's helpful, because if you go along with someone else's thought it's only going to get you so far. Because you don't know how they developed that thought, you don't know how they came to that, you don't know where they would go from that, so if you go on someone else's thinking, it makes it really hard to keep going with it. You don't even know how they got there, so if you develop your own thought, you know how you got there, you know what it is, and you know where you're going to go with it. In past classes, I've had people give me their answers—like a teacher—I'd ask them a question and they'd give me their answer—and I'd go off of it"—her fingers pantomime typing as she talks—"and my paper wouldn't be good because I'd have no—I wouldn't have a good conclusion, I wouldn't really have strong paragraphs after it, and it just all crumbled from there because I didn't go on my own thinking, which is a bad thing. So that's the one thing I'd say, let people develop their own ideas, not the teacher's. Don't give them your answer, give them theirs. It's hard to say, but let them develop their own thinking." (The video of Amelia's interview and one day of her group's discussion is on www.pennykittle.net under the videos tab.)

Wondering how you can lead students in analysis if you haven't read the book? This is not as big a problem as you may think. For one thing, when you ask students to talk in groups of three or four about their characters and what they're learning and how they're finding evidence to support their conclusions about character, you can wander among groups and listen in. You'll learn a lot about a lot of books as well as about how well your students are able to gather evidence to support their ideas.

But here's a more important truth: it is fine when students know more about their subject of study than we do. We have the strategies; they have the content. I can still teach the strategy in a conference. When a student tells me he is studying a character from a science fiction book I've never heard of, my questions won't be about who the character is and what the conflict is and what the other story elements are; they will center on thinking—the work we do as readers to analyze characters and their role in story. I might say, "So what do you know about this character and how do you know that? You need to find places in the text to support these conclusions you've drawn about your character. You know he has to develop courage, for example, to take on this role he is being pushed into, so where exactly in the text does he develop it?" It's about nudging a student toward independence. It's a thrill to see students own this work and embrace problem solving without online support.

Listen to a bit of what Aspen discovers after rereading *Wintergirls*:

> This novel was not written by the author, Laurie Halse Anderson, it was crafted by the artist. The unique stylistic quirks of the story let the readers into the unique mind of the teenage girl, Lia, a girl who edits her own thoughts and revises her own feelings. She is stuck in a place where reality doesn't exist; she doesn't have to eat, breathe, think. Lia

is frozen in a fantasy world that she created; living in her own mind. She is a wintergirl, stuck in the cold storm of anorexia, frozen and unable to thaw out.

Anderson doesn't only use creativity in the way she writes, but also in the style that she does it. One example of this is how she crosses out certain words throughout the book. I think the reason she did this is to show how Lia's mind works. Lia naturally has the urge to eat food but she tries to block it out and not let herself feel it, but every now and then the thoughts slip through her mental wall. "~~One bite, please, and then another and another, crust and cheese sausage sauce another and another~~ empty is strong and invincible." She won't let herself feel hungry because then she will be weak. She doesn't only block out her feelings about food but also about her parents. Instead of calling them Mom and Dad, she calls them Dr. Marrigan and Professor Overbrook. This says a lot about the way she feels about her parents. It could mean that she refers to them the same way other people do because she doesn't even feel like a daughter to them or it could mean that she thinks their jobs are more important to them than her, because they are always too busy for her. Her only way to deal with it all is to stay empty. Lia's life motto is empty = strong. Empty is clean and pure, rid of all bad. She may not be able to control the things happening in her life but she can control the food that goes into her mouth, or the lack thereof.

Numbers also play a big role in this book. Whether it be the amount of times her best friend called her before she died (33), or the numbers on the scale, or the body mass index of the person standing next to her, or the calories in that muffin, she is always counting. Lia uses numbers to get her mind off other things; if she is always counting then she can't think about the other problems in her life that are really bothering her. The author even made the number of each chapter look like the numbers a scale would read. I think she did this to show how everything in Lia's world revolves around her obsessive tracking of her weight. If she weighed 85, she'd want to get down to 80, then 75, 70, until nothing was left. She even mentions once in the book that her ideal weight would be 0.

"When I was a real girl . . ." is repeated many times throughout the book. Anderson usually follows it with a flashback of a nice family moment, or a fun time with her best friend, flashbacks of all the things that are broken now. I think the author did this to give the reader an idea of why Lia fell into anorexia, her life used to be so put together, and now everything has fallen apart and she doesn't know how to cope. The flashbacks are there to show the things that contributed to her not being able to be a real girl now. It shows how bad she wants to just have things go back to the way they were, but there is nothing that she can do to change it. I think she doesn't feel like a real girl because she can't live a normal life, her mind has to focus on being constantly in control of pushing away her desires and that has to be mentally wearing after awhile.

We must lead students to pay attention to the structure and complexity in fiction, analyzing and interpreting the moves of the author and the text. We have always done this work in English class, but this assignment allows me to push for the independence I know my students need.

I have also grown as a teacher by reading Jeff Anderson's work about imitating craft in sentences. My copies of his books *Mechanically Inclined* (2005) and *Everyday Editing* (2007) are well marked up. His newest, *Ten Things Every Writer Needs to Know* (2011), anchors the thinking I'll do with students this week on framing their research papers by studying beginnings and endings in nonfiction books. Figure 7.5 is a sample of sentence work in which my students wrote imitations of a sentence written by Maya Angelou.

Figure 7.5 *Sentence work sample*

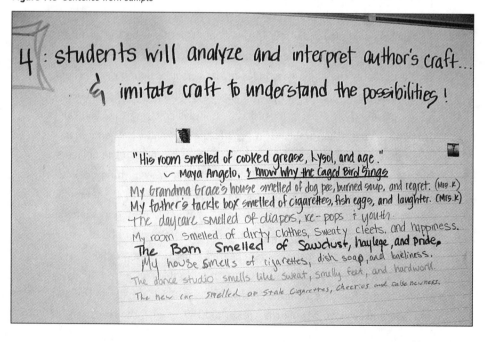

Another simple activity I use to prompt writing about reading is to ask students to find a sentence from something they've read recently that they love for the beauty of the language or what it tells them about life, then write what they're thinking in response. Students share these around their tables of four, reading the sentences others have chosen and immersing themselves in good writing and getting a peek at the books others are reading.

This week my favorite sentence is full of parallels. It comes from Jennifer E. Smith's *The Statistical Probability of Love at First Sight*: "And later, when it started to become clear that she cared more about soccer practice and phone privileges than Jane Austen or Walt Whitman, when the hour turned into a half hour and every night turned into every other, it no longer mattered" (152). I wrote the following in response in front of students: *In the spring of seventh grade, when it started to become clear that she cared more about basketball and tennis than a boyfriend or lip gloss, when she skipped the dance to watch a tournament and stopped returning phone calls, her friends shook their puzzled heads and grew up without her.*

I believe we grow as writers by standing on the shoulders (as Katie Wood Ray says) of those who write better than we do. I don't think this is plagiarism, I think it is part of our study of the craft of what we're reading.

Modeling Thinking About Themes

Books allow us to ponder important ideas and issues that don't have easy answers. We stumble along beside characters who are trying to determine the next best move. Sometimes a book reminds me that doing the right thing isn't always rewarded but I should keep trying because it matters. When I look for these larger connections with students, I show them how books share themes and ideas.

Here's an example. I pick two books from my own fall reading list, *The Sky Is Everywhere* and *Okay for Now*. I talk and write in front of my class:

> So I want to think more deeply about these two books that have
> had a lasting impact on me. I'm going to brainstorm the big ideas
> that struck me with each book:
>
> ### THE SKY IS EVERYWHERE
>
> falling in love
> mistakes we make
> the ways we deceive ourselves instead of facing what is hard
> how writing poetry is like bleeding to a hemorrhaging soul
> absent parents
> longing

OKAY FOR NOW

poverty and shame and how little power children have in their lives

art

brutality

forgiveness

friendship and first loves or crushes

how impossibly hard life is

Now I want to think about how these books are similar. I'm looking for connection and I'm using writing to help me discover deeper thinking. [*A student says, "First love."*] Yep, I see that. Now I want you to let me think in front of you without interrupting me. I want to model this process of finding connections by writing. This is the process of thinking I'm going to ask you to do in notebooks— alone—today, so let me puzzle through it alone now.

I see the connection in *first loves*, although they're really different because of the age of the characters. The first [*I point to* The Sky Is Everywhere] is like my experience falling in love for real verses [*I point to* Okay for Now] my crushes in middle and high school, but it wasn't love that kept me thinking about these books.

I'm going to leave that alone and look at the connection both books have to *longing*. I don't know what I should call it—or what the literary theme might be that I'm reaching for—but both books explore how characters adapt when they can't have what they want. Lennie's mother has been absent her entire life, and now she's lost her older sister and only sibling, so she spins in a confused place. And Doug has a brutal, violent father and a cowering mother and a longing to fit into his new town and school.

Suddenly I see a more important connection. They both have *art*. Lennie writes poems, which she leaves all over town, and Doug learns to draw at the local library. I want to think more about art as healing.

I think both books fit into the category of literature we call *coming of age*. Lennie and Doug are at different places in this process (middle and high school) but struggling with the same things that all people do as they pass from childhood to young adulthood.

But wait—I just thought of this. They both have the how-random-life-is theme going on that I noticed in a book I read last year. What do I make of that? The books could actually both go in a different category altogether. I'm not sure what yet. Not *death and dying* because no one dies in *Okay for Now*, but then again, maybe they could because one character's life is in jeopardy at the end of the book. Maybe they still fit in *coming of age* because they move to an understanding of mortality.

This is the kind of writing I want from you today: discovery drafting. Take two or possibly three books from your reading list and draw some connections. Imagine where the books fit into the ideas and categories or themes we've found in literature together. You can list and sketch or write in sentences. Later, we'll deepen our thinking by adding evidence for how the theme is revealed in each.

I prefer having students do this kind of writing about books they are reading independently, because when I ask questions about classic literature, I get too few honest, discovery-draft responses. Students seem compelled to say something literary, and since they don't trust their own incomplete understandings, they steal someone else's thinking so they'll have smart things to say. Also, too many of them haven't read the book, so how can they write honestly about it? I want my students to trust in their own incomplete understandings and thus develop a belief in discovery writing and their thinking about books.

Chapter 8

Nurturing Interdependent Readers in a Classroom Community

Synthesis is about organizing the different pieces to create a beautiful mosaic, a meaning, a beauty, greater than the sum of each shiny piece.

—*Ellin Keene*

Big Idea Books

I see possibility humming beneath reading workshop. My students make choices and read alone, but are connected within the classroom and throughout time to central themes in literature. The books they are reading cover a wide range of subjects and purposes but share common qualities. I created something I call "big idea books" to make those connections more obvious to my students. Here's how it works.

I buy cheap notebooks at an office supply store and label them with common themes in literature, one per notebook: *guilt; hope; fate; cruelty; isolation; justice; gender; freedom; coming of age; ambition; alienation; abandonment; conflict; suffering; yin & yang; the bonds of family; sacrifice; friendship; man struggling against nature/man/societal pressure to understand God; overcoming adversity; life lessons; empathy; change; courage; acceptance; love; death and dying; decisions; discipline; oppression; forgiveness;* and *belief*. I paste the following explanation on the inside cover of each notebook:

Big Idea Books

These notebooks are for us to share. I write in them; you write in them. A big idea book is a multiyear conversation, because I use them year after year. You're talking across time to students who are stumbling along through elementary or middle school right now but will one day sit where you are.

The meat of a big idea book is *your thinking*. I want you digging for what is beneath the story you're reading. You chose this book (this theme) for a reason. You can see how it connects to what is happening or what is explored in the book you're reading. You might connect the ideas or situations in the book to something in yourself or another book you've read. You might take the ideas in the book and go farther with them . . . thinking as you write.

You are doing a mini–book talk for someone who comes upon your words later. Try not to give away anything important that readers would rather discover on their own: you know how you hate that. You can skim a big idea book and find a dozen book talks from students like you. Add the titles to your to-read-next list, and you'll have a range of possibilities when you've finished one book and can't decide what to read next.

Rules for Civil Discourse in Community Writing

1. Be respectful. Do not use profanity. Do not use someone else's name without permission.

2. You only need to sign your entry if you want to. Sometimes we send words out into the world as a gift without attribution.

3. Trust the writer inside of you. Just write.

I cover the tables in my classroom with these books and watch students notice them as they settle into their seats. "Choose one," I say, "that connects somehow to the book you're reading right now." I pick up the notebook labeled *courage* and show them the book I finished the weekend before, *The Last True Story I'll Ever Tell: An Accidental Soldier's Account of the War in Iraq*, by John Crawford. "This memoir is all about courage. I want to think about the way courage resonates in this book. It's more than the courage of the soldiers, there are other ways to think about courage that I want to explore in freewriting."

As students browse the tables, I talk about themes with them and make superficial connections to the books they are reading, encouraging them to select a notebook, even if a theme/book relationship isn't yet clear to them. Within minutes all the students have a notebook and are back in their seats. We write for about ten minutes. The last class of the day has the best experience. They often find one or two entries from other students (see the examples in Figures 8.1, 8.2, 8.3, and 8.4); reading them helps them think and their writing comes easier.

My intention is not to burden reading with activity. The purpose of personal reading is joy, curiosity, and interest—the kinds of things that are the foundation of my own reading life. But I also want students to stop once in awhile, step back from the story, and dig into what is happening underneath. I believe this will bring them more pleasure in the book and in the act of reading. Big idea books help my students do this, and they help me understand what I might teach next.

Figure 8.1 *Suffering*/Columbine

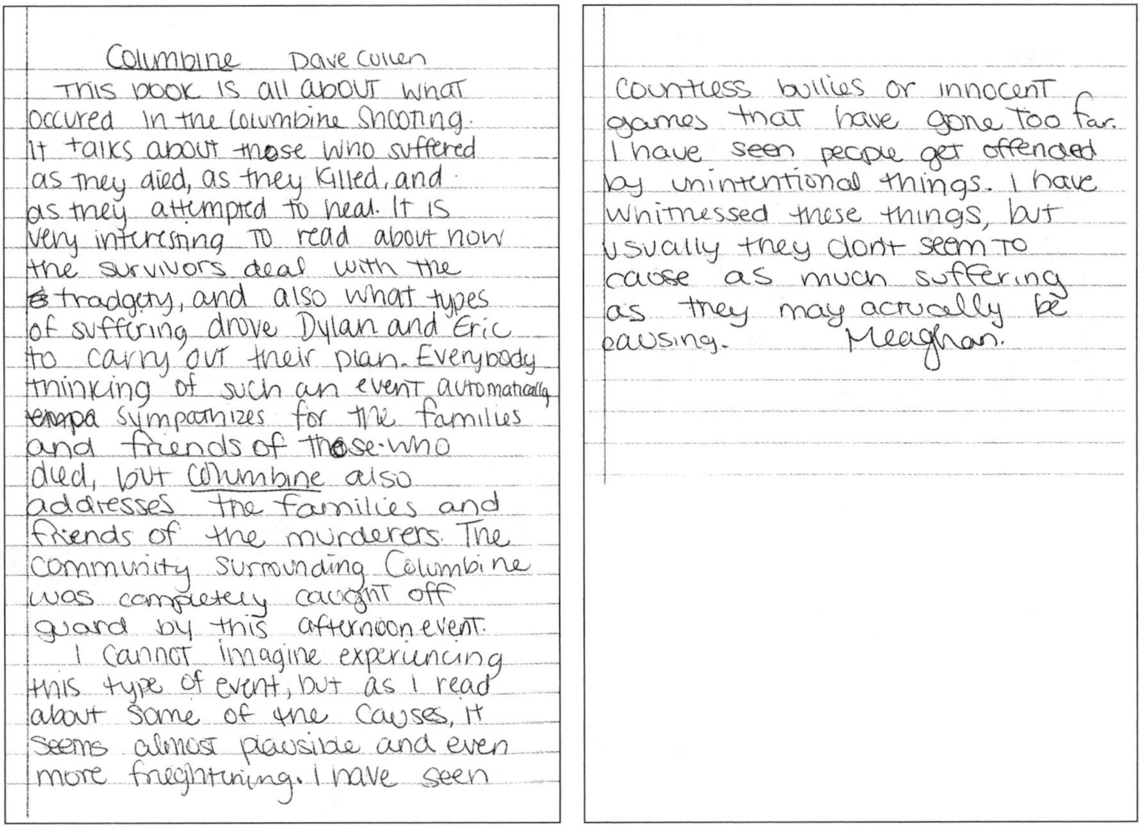

Columbine   Dave Cullen
This book is all about what occured in the Columbine Shooting. It talks about those who suffered as they died, as they killed, and as they attempted to heal. It is very interesting to read about how the survivors deal with the tradgety, and also what types of suffering drove Dylan and Eric to carry out their plan. Everybody thinking of such an event automatically sympathizes for the families and friends of those who died, but Columbine also addresses the families and friends of the murderers. The community surrounding Columbine was completely caught off guard by this afternoon event.
I cannot imagine experiencing this type of event, but as I read about some of the causes, it seems almost plausible and even more freightning. I have seen

countless bullies or innocent games that have gone too far. I have seen people get offended by unintentional things. I have whitnessed these things, but usually they don't seem to cause as much suffering as they may actually be causing.   Meaghan.

An "Order" for Literature

By conferring with individual readers and reading their notebook entries we begin to see where they are as readers. But we want more than just a collection of individual satellites. We want a solar system, a community of readers working together to understand the entire field of literature better. Can we connect readers to a greater understanding of purposes and passions in books throughout history, as well as to one another? This expansive thinking can only be accomplished when students are engaged in a reading journey, not just a particular book.

I want my students' personal reading to have a purpose. I expect all my students to craft a reading life through their individual choices over time (the school year and beyond). My goal is for every reader to understand the limitless possibilities of literature.

Figure 8.2 *Oppression*/Unbroken

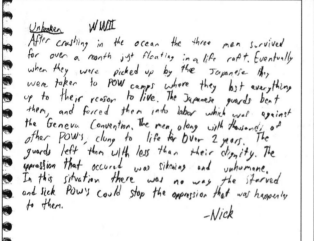

Unbroken   WWII

After crashing in the ocean the three men survived for over a month just floating in a life raft. Eventually when they were picked up by the Japanese they were taken to POW camps where they lost everything up to their reason to live. The Japanese guards beat them, and forced them into labor which was against the Geneva Convention. The men, along with thousands of other POW's, clung to life for over 2 years. The guards left them with less than their dignity. The oppression that occured was sikening and unhumone. In this situation there was no way the starved and sick POW's could stop the oppression that was happening to them.

—Nick

Figure 8.3 *Freedom*/*The White Tiger*

The White Tiger   by Aravind Adiga

This whole book is centered around a driver. Although his job is to cart around his masters, the job came with other duties. He is technically a servant in their house, doing anything that needs to be done. So far, the author tells you that he has killed his master and went onto bigger and better things. You could say he achieved freedom. The author describes that in India, everyone is, in some way, a servant to someone else. A driver is considered very well off, but is still considered a servant. The masters of all these servants are the "landlords" that control different parts of India. Everyone serves them, all the time. Anyways, the driver in the story talks about the lavoshes of his new found freedom.

This approach to teaching literature requires a shift in thinking about teaching reading in general. Teaching reading is not imparting knowledge to a reader about a particular book; rather, it is using a deep understanding of ways of knowing *many* books to nudge a reader to another place in his or her thinking about, first, an individual book and then about literature as a whole.

This requires a classification of sorts, an order of books that helps students see connections. Prompting students' thinking by way of inquiry, not direct teaching, is the essence of education. Students remember what they do and what they discover, not what they are told.

Let me show you what I mean using my own experience with science. I was studying astronomy one night with three best friends, all engineering majors, during sophomore year at Oregon State. I was memorizing notes, but I still couldn't see how the universe worked. Finally Bob stood up (6'2" legs in Levis and a killer

Figure 8.4 *Man's Struggles*/A Brief History of Time

A Breifer History of Time, Steven Hawkens
Well This book is more about mans struggle to understand the univers, but since many people still believe in god and the fact that god created the universe, the author does make a few comments regarding gods intcasions. If God is real than he could have set up the universe in anyway he wanted, but only if he set it up in a few way could we have RXisted today. And to add to that, Once the universe was set up you could think of it as gods child, it is free to grow and expand on its own without the interference of god. These ideas were created to nedge science with religion; science can only explan the universe from now to when it begans, but what was there before the universe begans?
                                    —Dalton

smile—believe me, he had my full attention) and said, "Paul, you be the sun," and started spinning—orbiting—around him. "I'm the Earth," he grinned at me, as Chris jumped up to orbit him.

"And Chris is the moon—oh, my god, I *get* it." I dropped my head in my hands. It was obvious, but it had never been clear *to me*. Although this moment was endlessly entertaining to my friends, I didn't mind that much because it launched me from one place to another as a science student.

Senior year I needed one more elective. I chose Oceanography because of my love of fishing, but during the first class I realized the content, the professor and his impossible expectations, and a room of Ocean Science majors would be hazardous to my GPA. I don't like to fail, but I don't like to back down, either. I didn't drop Oceanography. I created three thousand flash cards to help me learn the required terms and classifications and the order of the species, studying hours and hours until I passed the course. By midsummer I'd forgotten almost all those memorized terms. Of course I did. In fact, I never used 90 percent of that learning again. But I sit here decades later thinking about how that deep study changed the way I think; now I don't see things as individual parts as much as I seek connections between them. What I learned in Oceanography is that all species are connected through a complex order and classification. I seek that thinking in all things now, even in literature.

I create an "order" for literature across the back wall of my classroom that shows how all the books we're reading connect to one another across time, space, and genre—almost like a map of book talks but one in which my students name and order the connections. "Here's Shakespeare and over there are the Transcendentalists and there are the Romantics. Here we might put *Falling for Hamlet* and other modern adaptations of Will's work but also Ellen Hopkins' books, perhaps, because they tell stories in verse—can you name how they might be connected? Here are the Brontës and their brave voices in an age of censure. Who are their modern equivalents? Who writes what cannot be said today? I'd add Julie Anne Peters, author of *By the Time You Read This I'll Be Dead* and *Keeping You a Secret*. Who are some others?" Suddenly we're talking about ideas and authors' intentions. My students' thinking expands to meet the thinking of others in the room.

This map changes shape during the year as students learn more and think differently. I lead students to see their reading choices as worthy of study, yes, and as a part of something larger—a world of literature they don't yet know. I want to empower them to discern how ideas have been explored in books for centuries.

Drawing connections between ways of knowing the world and the thinking kids are doing about individual books is powerful teaching. It is so much deeper than studying one book in isolation. Listening to other readers, we see how their intentions in reading (and writing) are mostly about self-discovery, that the map of one person's reading life can't be traced over another's. Yet we are connected. Seeing their reading as part of a larger whole helps students make informed choices and deepen their understanding of and respect for things they may have dismissed in the past.

Literature allows a flexibility in thinking that just isn't possible in science. No scientist would accept my reordering of the species. He would scoff at my categories—Fish I Like to Catch (perch, casting from shore; steelhead; spring Chinook salmon; rainbow trout), Fish That Scare Me (sturgeon, all sizes; the 52-pound salmon my dad hauled in one fall; nasty-looking bottom-feeders)—you get the idea. My categories would be personal, not scientific, and that would bother a Serious Scientist. My students, likewise, connect books in ways that bother this British Literature Major: I cringe at what they're missing that I think is important, perhaps, but it is more important that they think in terms of their own connections triggered by their own understandings, not mine. When they argue about where a book fits in the order, they're using evidence from their thinking to make their point. I can then teach into their intentions as readers, adding what they don't know about the expansive field of literature.

I tread carefully. Students need to be the ones doing the thinking. As students analyze their reading choices by adding them to our classification, they'll see big ideas, or themes, in books and they'll see times when they read to follow one passion or one author (like Ethan through Kerouac and then Faulkner). I hope they'll see gaps, because they may not be aware of how narrow their choices are until they see expansiveness and possibility.

"Mind the gap" is not just a phrase I stole from the London Underground but a way to consider complexity that is different from simply increasing difficulty. I want students to analyze the gaps in the genres they read—to consider what they haven't read and why: "You've read from the life-in-high-school section of our classroom library for months, isn't it time to consider biography or poetry or the classics?" I can't get many students to read Walt Whitman's *Leaves of Grass* through a book talk, but if a collection of poetry from Iraq War veterans is the gateway to a poetry classification that includes Whitman, sometimes a poem like "Haddock of Mass Destruction" can lead a student to "Song of Myself." They see Walt on the map and ask, "Who is that again?" If students are willing to look at their reading gaps and consider why they are there, perhaps they'll work to bridge them, deepen their experience with a different period of literature or author, or simply see books as vast and worthy of exploration.

Perhaps is critical. I resist the temptation to determine what is next for my students, because my focus is on readers' forging a path toward deeper understanding. It is the journey that lasts, not necessarily the particular books.

Quarterly Reading Reflections

My school year is divided into quarters. At the end of each marking period, I ask my students to look back over their work as readers and analyze what they've done and what they can challenge themselves to do next. This quarterly reflection includes a reading-rate calculation as impacted by difficulty, interest, and genre. Students evaluate where they are and what they need to do to meet their target number of books, both fiction and nonfiction, for the year.

I believe in the power of setting goals and making them public. Don Murray used to send me his daily word counts; Don Graves forwarded me his daybook notes. It was inherently frustrating: I could never keep up. Those emails weren't for me, though; they kept the two of them accountable to themselves by making their personal goals public. My students need to understand why and how to challenge themselves as readers, to set goals, and then be nudged to commit to them.

Goals are more than just setting a target number of books to read during the year. I use Teri Lesesne's (2010) *Reading Ladders* to clarify increasing text complexity with my students. I put this problem on the board: how can a reader move from *Twilight* to *Dracula*? Right now that student is stuck on vampire fiction, I tell them, but let's imagine she wants to be a stronger reader. And frankly, who doesn't want to be? Really? Even my most reluctant students would like to be better readers. I think all people seek greater competence unless we don't believe we can get there and give up.

Take curling. You probably caught a few hours of the coverage during the most recent winter Olympics. You saw people with brooms chasing big rocks to the shouts of "Sweep!" Curious, to be sure; ridiculous, really—but stop by North Conway on a Saturday night and I'm out there with my fellow curlers sending stones into the "house." Well, I'm trying to anyway. I'm working to get better at it. Like any sport, curling is a combination of finesse and discipline. You have to learn the basics and work at them and then challenge yourself to learn more. I don't want to be bad at this. I want to be dazzling.

But learning is slow. Last week when I sent a stone down the ice, my husband—our skip (leader)—was standing in one place and my stone went somewhere else. When I lined up for the next throw he called down the ice, "Aim!"

My response was fiery. Why? Because I was *trying* to aim. I didn't know what to do to get better. I needed coaching, not just demands that I improve. I think of Keith. He said about his reading in ninth, tenth, and eleventh grades, "I tried to read [the assigned books] all the time. But I just couldn't do it. I couldn't like interpret what the words were saying." Telling Keith he isn't trying hard enough, as some have done, doesn't help him understand.

If you made me compete week after week against the best curlers in our league, I would soon tire of being the worst one. My ego couldn't take it. I'm good at other things, so I'd stop trying to keep up with those curlers. I'd make derisive comments about them on the sidelines. If I don't believe I can get better, practicing my throwing is a waste of time. Many students who hate reading have given up believing they can improve, partly because they are always in competition with stronger readers in the room, all using the same text, and partly because there is little teaching of reading strategies in high school. Reading ladders help students imagine a path that can lead to understanding more difficult texts independently. To get them there I use conferences and whole-class teaching of mentor texts to improve skills.

I require my students to consider these questions each quarter: *What makes reading difficult for you right now? How will you work to improve?* They prepare their reviews following a specified series of steps.

Step 1: Determine Difficulty

It starts with books. I ask students to work in small groups to answer this question, "How can you measure the difficulty of the books you've read this quarter?" I put a pile of books on the table. Their task is to order them from least to most difficult using whatever criteria makes sense to them. I listen in. Many start with the total number of pages, but quickly adjust that: the 550 pages in *The Invention of Hugo Cabret* require less of a reader per page than the 180 pages in *The Great Gatsby* do. They know books differ in sentence length and vocabulary from my minilessons on how to work through reading challenges, but they also know their interest in the book, often based on their own background knowledge of the subject, is a very important factor. The reading seems easier if the book captivates them. (The hockey memoir *Eleven Seconds* was hard for Abby and easy for Matt, but Matt couldn't imagine getting through Abby's favorite *Crazy in Love: The Beyoncé Knowles Biography.*) When we gather back as a class, we make a list of criteria, and students apply them to their own reading during the first quarter of the year. A recent class' criteria are shown in Figure 8.5.

Figure 8.5 *What makes a book difficult?*

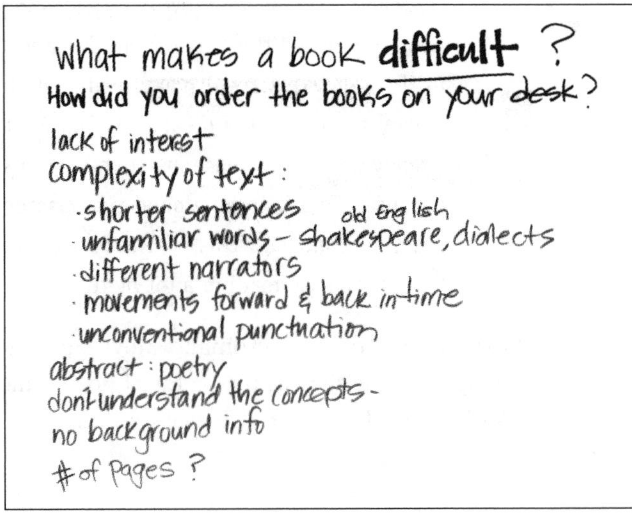

My first attempt to teach this ranking procedure didn't go well. (Too often I'm in a rush to save time and I miss the learning and processing that students need to do in order to own the thinking of a concept.) I walked in with a list of qualities that make books difficult and asked my students to order the books they had read from most to least difficult. This is assignment-driven, helicopter teaching. I was a master of hovering that day. I rushed around the room reexplaining directions and answering questions. Frustration mounted. Why didn't they get this? A concept doesn't live in us because we've read its definition. We must own the thinking behind it. When I put piles of books on desks and ask students to define the differences, they have time to work through their thinking and understand complexity in reading before they have to apply that thinking to the books they have read this quarter. (This same analysis is effective for determining the qualities of skillful writing as Nancie Atwell [1988] and Linda Rief [1991] have shown.)

Students reshuffle the criteria in the second, third, and fourth quarters. As they compile these lists I confer with them individually, puzzling over questions. *What have you read that has challenged you as a reader this quarter? How have you improved this quarter? What will you reach for next?* Figure 8.6 is Dalton's fourth-quarter list incorporating the previous three quarters.

Step 2: Determine Reading Rate

Students calculate the pages they read each week for the quarter based on the total number of pages they've read in nine weeks. This helps them pay attention to the reading they've done outside class, identify areas of needed improvement, and celebrate gains.

Here's Brittany's reflection on her first-quarter reading rate:

> My reading rate is very low (674 pages in 9 weeks) because, well, the two
> books I finished this quarter are probably the first full books I have read
> in three or five years. I never read much to begin with so this rate for me
> is very surprising and great and I am proud to see I am actually reading.
> I really want to increase my stamina and start to read a whole lot more
> because I find it to be a good time passer or just something to relax
> with. For right now this is already a big difference for me, but I would
> like to increase reading a lot more.

I expect more than two romance novels in a quarter from Brittney as a reader, but during this time she has read a lot of poetry and literature in class as well. Although it's vital that I increase Brittney's reading independence, students teach me again

Figure 8.6 *Dalton's reading ladder*

DALTON L'HEUREUX'S READING LADDER: QUARTERS 1–4

Books Read (Most Difficult to Least Difficult)

> * = Quarter 2 Additions
> ** = Quarter 3 Additions
> *** = Quarter 4 Additions

1. * *Runner's World: The Runner's Body*, 380 pp.
2. ** *The Pacific* by Hugh Ambrose, 449 pp. (actually read 30)
3. *A Walk in the Woods* by Bill Bryson, 392 pp.
4. ** *Extremely Loud & Incredibly Close* by Jonathon Foer, 420 pp.
5. * *Unbroken* by Laura Hillenbrand, 406 pp.
6. ** *A Briefer History of Time* by Steven Hawking, Kindle (386 pp.)
7. *Born to Run* by Christopher McDougall, 352 pp.
8. *** *50/50* by Dean Karnazes, 279 pp.
9. *** *The Good Soldiers* by David Finkel, 304 pp. (currently reading 25 pp.)
10. *The Hunger Games* by Suzanne Collins, 374 pp.
11. * *Catching Fire* by Suzanne Collins, 384 pp.
12. * *Mockingjay* by Suzanne Collins, 394 pp.
13. *Ranger's Apprentice: Erak's Ransom* by John Flanagan, 364 pp.
14. *Ranger's Apprentice: Knights of Conmel* by John Flanagan, 348 pp.
15. *Ranger's Apprentice: Halt's Pearl* by John Flanagan, 387 pp.
16. *** *Ranger's Apprentice: #10* by John Flanagan, ? pp. (next read)
17. *Percy Jackson and the Olympians: The Last Olympian* by Riordan, 394 pp.
18. ** *Winter's End* by Jean-Claude Mourlevat, 414 pp.
19. *** *The Maze Runner* by James Dashner, 398 pp.
20. *** *The Scorch Trials* by James Dashner, Kindle (380 pp.)
21. *I Am the Messenger* by Markus Zusak, 379 pp.
22. ** *Boot Camp* by Todd Strasser, 314 pp.
23. * *The Absolutely True Diary of a Part-Time Indian* by Sherman Alexie, 230 pp.

Why this order? Bill Bryson's *A Walk in the Woods* was the most challenging book I read. The font was small and a lot was crammed into a page; you really had to pay attention to him when he was explaining historical sites or facts about how the world is deteriorating. *Born to Run* was my second hardest read; I often lost track of what was going on much in the same way as I did with *A Walk in the Woods*. *The Hunger Games* comes next in line, not because it's challenging, but because it took me a few chapters to get used to Collins' writing and how she words phrases. The Ranger's Apprentices books and *Percy Jackson* came next. The reading was easy and I flew through the books. However I find more of our vocab words within Ranger's Apprentice books than in any other piece of writing. The first book I read this year was also the easiest, seems reasonable enough.

and again to start where they are and nudge them forward. What's important is that Brittney is reading regularly and wants "to increase her stamina and start to read a whole lot more." If she wants it, my work is possible.

Getting to slow, deep, and still pleasurable reading is not going to happen quickly for students who have been faking it for years. Some spend weeks finding books that interest them enough for that kind of investment. Some spend weeks trying to figure out whether I'm serious about turning them into habitual readers. Will I notice? Will I keep pressuring them? Until they're into crafting their own reading lives, they won't be looking for challenges. Sometimes this takes so long, I despair that they ever will. And sometimes they don't—and that breaks my book-loving heart. However, when students are surrounded by peers who are chasing challenges, it starts to infect them. Monique picked up *The Kite Runner* partly because she noticed what other advanced kids were reading and partly because she was finally ready to challenge herself.

Step 3: Write Minireviews of Favorite Books

I ask students to summarize a few books they loved, not only because summarization is an essential writing skill (Graham and Perin 2007), but because when they're finished I'll have oodles of book talks for student to share with one another. Tristin wrote:

> Of all the books I have read this quarter, *The Places in Between* has been the most difficult, at least based on language and content. Fortunately, I enjoyed reading it and found the story he told intriguing. Unlike *Water for Elephants*, whose plot really didn't interest me very much, *The Places in Between* was able to keep me reading because I like the idea he had and wanted to learn more about the culture. I was distraught when his dog died and indeed I feared for his life at times, though clearly he had to survive. While this book was one of my slowest reads, it was also one of my most rewarding.

He has compared the two books, but he hasn't summarized either one. I had assumed he knew what I expected in a summary, but after reading a pile of reading ladders I realize he is not alone. I bring several student summaries to class the next day and we analyze them together to identify the elements of an effective summary. Here's one of the samples we studied:

> The world we know it has been destroyed, and a central government, known as the Capitol, has risen to power as a dictator over the remaining districts in North America in Suzanne Collins' *The Hunger Games*. As a

punishment for the districts' rebellion years back against the Capitol, the Capitol holds the annual Hunger Games. The Hunger Games is a competition when a boy and a girl from each of the 12 districts between the ages of 12 and 18 compete in an arena set up by the Capitol, where winning means fame and food, and losing means death.

It's not perfect, but it models elements I'm looking for. When I combine this example with a few others, students are able to identify the qualities of an effective summary and then revise their own.

Step 4: Set Goals

Many educators have emphasized the need for students to set personal goals and work toward them, monitoring their own progress (see Marzano, Pickering, and Pollock 2001). This investment in learning is critical. Each quarter each student sets goals in reading, both volume and complexity. Students' goals are as individual as they are. Some make a list of books they want to read. Others challenge themselves to increase the difficulty of their reading. At the end of the second quarter Dalton wrote:

> All goals for quarter 2 completed. This is more reading than I've done in my entire life combined. I am not struggling with the amount, but I do not plan on turning it into a struggle. I've read a good number of pages, and I'm content with where I am. I don't read a wide variety of books so maybe I can try out different genres, but probably not. I hope to start reading things a little more challenging, just not so challenging that it's no longer fun.
>
> I read two challenging books that took me a while to get through. I did a good job widening my reading selection; I'm now enjoying informative books and true stories instead of just fiction. The amount of reading I'm doing is not coming from force, so that's good and I plan on just continuing to read.

At the end of the third quarter he wrote:

> I have blown my reading rate to smithereens this quarter and I intend to do the same next quarter. I want to read some harder books that will challenge me to think more when I read.

I sent Dalton back to specify titles he would commit to reading that would challenge him.

Step 5: Reflect on Your Reading in a Short Essay

I revise what I ask for in this reflection each time I use it, and I post the current questions on my website (pennykittle.net) each quarter. Here are excerpts from three student reflections:

Student 1

Reading is not really easy. This is so true and is an idea that statistics do not take into account. Statistics don't counter for the fact that about nine out of ten books are really, really bad. Of course, this is just one opinion, but as a senior, I watch every day as my classmates give up on their books and get frustrated with reading because there are so many books out there to choose from, and it's always a gamble to pick a good one. I think a lot more people would read if they had books that related to them and interested them. I've been shocked at the rate that fellow classmates, typically nonreaders, fly through certain books when they find one they like, and often times during other classes I look up to see them not paying attention to the teacher, but READING. How exciting!

Student 2

Choice is a very important aspect in life. Choosing to work and save money or to spend everything you make. Or choosing to devote yourself to school or to party and slack off. Choice is how we live our lives, so why should we be given choice in the books we read? Being given choice in what we read is highly beneficial to students.

Take me for example. Before this year I was always assigned books to read by my teachers. The library I was assigned, with a few exceptions, was extremely boring; therefore I rarely divulged in reading. Then this year rolled around, and I was given choice. At first I was a little intimidated by the choice, but then I started thinking this could be a good challenge. I started this year off with *Hunger Games*, which I thoroughly enjoyed. I then continued on to read another nine books in three quarters. Wow, ten books. Ten books were more than I had fully read in the three years prior. I would not have read even close to that had I been assigned more boring books to read. Choice was a helpful aspect in making me a more frequent reader.

Those who are against choice would argue that students may simply read "low-level" books the entire year and never challenge themselves. This would fail to prepare students adequately for college reading. Well, let us look at my reading list once again. Yes, the first few books I read were not too challenging; I just needed to start reading. After these few books, however, I read *Slaughterhouse Five* by choice. This novel was actually one assigned by some teachers in the building. After *Slaughterhouse Five* I took on a huge challenge. I began to read *Crime and Punishment*, again, by choice. Other students in my class have also challenged themselves with other novels like *Lolita* and *Unbroken*. So to all the naysayers, even with choice, students will challenge themselves and prepare themselves for college.

When it comes to reading, choice is critical. It will get those students who don't read to start reading and will keep the students who read, reading. In my case, choice has been extremely helpful in getting me to start reading, as well as begin to challenge myself in my reading. Without choice I would be continuing my trend from years past and not reading at all.

Student 3

Can you imagine being *A Long Way Gone* from home, having *Tuesdays with Morrie*, getting *Water for Elephants* at the circus, being a bike racer and being told *It's Not About the Bike*, being the greatest *Kite Runner* in your town or perhaps *Sold* into child prostitution? I couldn't or at least not until I read these books. Book after book, page after page, my journey through life gained depth. I started this semester as a woman growing up in the early 30s and quickly realized I just wasn't getting what I needed from that, and so I began having *Tuesdays with Morrie*, learning the most about something feared by everyone: death. I then became an autistic child reading *The Curious Incident of the Dog in the Nightime*. I was a little boy, trying to uncover a murder while I lived with this uncontrollable condition. I then stepped into the center ring and became a veterinarian in charge of getting *Water for Elephants*. I was caught in a love triangle aboard a moving train, wishing that it would just stop. This book was brilliant and is now at the top of my favorites list. I learned about Lance Armstrong's battle with cancer and chemotherapy, continuing on in his dream to win the Tour de France. I climbed hills and passed through small villages with crowds cheering me on. I wore the yellow jersey of a winner. From there I became a child soldier, and a boy growing up in a third world country trying to please his father, ending my semester in child prostitution.

I took the place of every main character. I lived the lives of other people, opening my mind more and more to the world around me. I am enjoying reading more than ever and I've adopted the habit of dropping books I'm not enjoying. I disliked reading about *The Lone Ranger and Tonto Fistfight in Heaven* or how *A Tree Grows in Brooklyn*. I could never take the place of the main character in those books. I have, however, realized that sometimes you just have to grab a book and start reading. The title might not be catchy, and the cover might not be too splashy, but sometimes that's when you find the words the most enthralling. I love page turners and "unputdownables" and I knew that if I wasn't reading one of those, I probably wouldn't get as much out of it.

Not only have I lived the lives of a dozen or so different people, I have opened the door to a great reading habit, enabling me to become hundreds of more people with the turn of a page. I have learned about styles of writing used, especially the ones that I enjoy reading, and that has shown up in my writing. I have been able to take steps in my writing that I normally wouldn't have.

Reading nearly 2,483 pages this semester, I feel as if I have gained more knowledge about the world than I have just about writing. I have officially become a reader, not just a "this is my assigned book this month, what chapters am I reading tonight" reader.

Reading Lives That Last

~*~*~

You need to make acts of art of the very acts of life.

—David Citino

The student with me in the above photo is Kristen. In the past I've suggested (in *Write Beside Them*, 2008) that she learned to write because her profanity earned her so many lunch detentions in my office, where I could teach her. I was the sheriff, and she just didn't respect the badge. Rule breakers need some discipline, you know, so we spent hours together. Hours. There are people in my life who find this ironic: my son, Cam, who taught his friend how to spell the *f*-word in kindergarten so they could both use it in their writing; my friends who wince and shake their heads or trade entertaining, offensive remarks with me; and my principal, who began issuing fines when I used my favorite words in meetings. I know, I know, such a hypocrite I am. They're wonderfully ambidextrous words, but that doesn't mean I let my students use them.

I've always thought those lunch detentions were a gift for both Kristen and me. I taught her mechanics and helped her find moments in her notebook that told the stories she needed to tell. She became more confident and skillful in her writing, earned our school's "most improved" award at graduation, and went off to college that fall.

Kristen and I met for coffee yesterday. She is almost six years out of high school, and this spring she'll finish her degree at a community college. We hope.

You know what we talked about? Books.

I've been rethinking her story. Stephen Krashen (1993) said, "There is strong evidence that free voluntary reading is effective in developing literacy. Those who read more read better, write better, spell better, and develop better grammatical competence and larger vocabularies." I think back to our semester together that winter and spring of her senior year and remember Kristen's deep concentration during silent reading. I remember how quickly she moved through books. I didn't give that the credit I should have. I've been paying better attention to reading in my courses since then, and I see its impact on her writing so clearly now.

Kristen had read one book in high school before she came to me, *The Catcher in the Rye*. I told her she could read anything, but she had no idea what to read. She wasn't just going to start reading; none of my nonreaders will. They need a teacher who reads, who says, "Kristen, you'd love this, I think. Or this. Or this. Just try it." And my students need a teacher who won't quit nudging, suggesting, and believing in them.

So as Kristen and I sat smiling at each other, watching a sleety rain coat the parking lot at Starbucks, I asked her what I always ask former students, "What are you reading?" She has come by my office or emailed me dozens of times since she graduated. I'm always sending her out the door with this book or this one or this one ("Seriously, Kristen, you'll *love* it"). Today I told her about *Makes Me Wanna Holler*, which challenged my thinking in dozens of ways. It's a powerful memoir, Kristen's preferred genre. I said, "Stop by, it's in my room, but I haven't convinced any of my students to read it. It's long and difficult."

"Nah," she shrugged, "I'll buy it. I like to own my books."

She told me about her bookshelf "as tall as that one"—she nodded at the shelf across the coffee shop—"and it's full. People don't think I'm a reader. They're always saying, 'You read?' and I say, 'I've read all of these.' I like having them." She's read every day since we parted that June, finishing more than 250 books, she told me.

I asked her what made her a reader.

"It was *The Burn Journals*," she answered immediately, "that was the book."

That's a tough book, an impossibly tough book. A boy determines to end his life, so he steps into the shower in a bathrobe, soaks himself in lighter fluid, and sets himself on fire. The book is the story of his recovery, one painful skin graft after another. When I finished reading it, I wasn't even sure I would bring it into my room. There aren't many students who want to take that journey, but Kristen did. And as she read it, she suddenly realized that books could be relevant. That books had power.

Kristen has had impossibly tough things in her life. There are stories she's only hinted at but I know haunt her. She told me that most of the books her teachers gave her in high school had nothing to do with her, so she had nothing to do with them. And we sweep that aside as if how a book speaks to a reader is not the most important part of reading. As if because someone says a particular book is important, it is important for everyone.

Really?

I have some colorful language to share in response to that.

We can't create readers with books that are miles from the lives and experiences of the kids in the chairs around us. And creating readers, creating students who are still reading when you meet them six years later, that's what my work is for.

Kristen has struggled with college. She's struggled to make time for it: she works full-time, always has, always will. College courses are wedged into the hours between driving to the campus, running the bakery at our local grocery store, observing in schools for her education major, and writing all those papers she finds useless and frustrating. She's had no trouble keeping reading in that mix. The only hurdle is finding the right books. She browses bookstores, listens to readers, and contacts her old teacher for suggestions.

Books will continue to guide, enlighten, and joyfully share her life. Someday Kristen will teach, and she will pass on this love of reading. Lucky students.

Chapter **9**

Creating a School Community of Readers

Children of poverty have practically nothing to read. More access to books results in more reading. More reading results in more literacy development.

—*Stephen Krashen*

How Standardized Measures Fail Us

How do we measure what our students are able to do as readers? My school district has a menu of tests that are administered regularly in individual schools, in all district schools, and as part of a New England compact of schools. Then we add national tests (NAEP, SAT) to be sure taxpayers can compare us in as many ways as they might wish to. Soon we'll have the Common Core tests. None of our local or national tests measure the joy students take in reading or their stamina for it. None measure our ability to create lifelong readers in thirteen years of schooling. Those are critical, haunting omissions.

You might be tempted to call the SAT and similar tests a measure of stamina simply because a student must read long passages quickly in order to answer questions. It takes stamina to read, focus, and respond for hours at a time, of course, but the SAT will not reveal whether a student can read uninterrupted for thirty minutes or more on one topic, deepening their thinking and understanding. That kind of stamina is a necessary component of an intellectual life. It is necessary in most professions, and it would add much to our democratic process. And we don't measure it.

We have too many readers who skim, who do not slow down to think. This is not about the content students prefer—Facebook, YouTube, etc.—or whether they use the web for homework or not. It is about the reading styles they employ. As Mark Bauerlein notes:

> They race across the surface, dicing language and ideas into bullets and graphics, seeking what they already want and shunning the rest. They convert history, philosophy, literature, civics, and fine art into information, material to retrieve and pass along.
>
> That's the drift of screen reading. Yes, it's a kind of literacy, but it breaks down in the face of dense argument, a modernist poem, a long political tract, and other texts that require steady focus and linear attention—in a word, slow reading. Fast scanning doesn't foster flexible minds that can adapt to all kinds of texts, and it doesn't translate into academic reading. If it did, then in a 2006 *Chronicle of Higher Education* survey of college professors, 41 percent wouldn't have labeled students "not well prepared" in reading (48 percent rated them "somewhat well prepared").
>
> We would see reading scores inching upward, instead of seeing, for instance, that the percentage of high school students who reached proficiency dropped from 40 percent to 35 percent between 1992 and 2005. (2008, 2)

Standardized tests can't measure this kind of reading, but a classroom teacher can. We know who among our students likes to read and who finds no joy in it. But what do we do with that information? Has anyone asked us to consider the importance of that question and address it? If we don't collect information on key things readers must do, how do we know what to do next?

If we can understand how our standardized measures fail us and fail our students, perhaps we can design better ones. Here is an (incomplete) list of failings I see in current assessment practices:

1. Speed reading is of little value in the world, yet speed is at the center of standardized testing and the reason many students do poorly. I've read that in order for students to be successful on the ACT, they need to be able to read each passage in eight minutes. Slow reading, as Tom Newkirk (2011) has articulated, leads to deeper comprehension. Where do we measure slow, focused attention?

2. People position standardized tests as authoritative indications of a child's knowledge, skill, and educational progress. What about parents? Parents have an intuitive sense of what matters—"he used to love reading, now he hates it"—and can help us see a reader and his needs more accurately,

but they are being told that what they know doesn't matter. If we return parents and teachers to a partnership in an assessment of reading we'll learn much more.

3. We do not have a standardized measure for resiliency. What process do readers use when they can't understand? Errors teach us. Can students articulate the moves that distinguish a first reading from a closer, better one? This is a skill they need to be able to analyze complex texts beyond high school.

4. Standardized tests can give us a false sense of security about what students are able to do as readers. A boy in my ninth-grade class this year scored proficient on the NECAP assessment in eighth grade so is not being given reading assistance in high school, but he has not finished a book this year (it is late March) and struggles to explain his understanding of even short articles from the newspaper.

5. We want students to love reading and read for the rest of their lives. There is nothing in a standardized test that measures this or lets us know whether we're close to reaching that goal.

6. Test scores are being used to condemn an entire school or system based on the poor performance of a few students. But even more important, people believe these tests actually measure who can read. I remember a businessman ranting about the results of our school district's third-grade tests one year: "I can't believe 32 percent of our third graders can't read!" I countered, "No one listened to any of those kids read and asked them if they understood. That's not what tests do. We get real information about reading by sitting in classrooms beside our students, not from tests." The problem, of course, is that in a secondary teacher's schedule of five or more classes and 150 or more students, the practice of sitting beside students, listening to them read, and discussing their understanding is simply not happening enough.

7. International comparisons fail to give us good information about reading. To understand how American students compare with the rest of the world, we should remember we are not testing the same populations. In the United States we still believe in educating 100 percent of our youth to adulthood; yes, we are failing to do that, but many countries are not even trying. Many countries send only students bound for college on to secondary schools. What are we comparing?

8. In far too many cases standardized test scores do not match what the students can do independently. Tricks that allow students to master the conditions of the test rather than the material mask students' real

problems. The reality that teachers and school leaders "teach to the test" is distressing. It reflects the pressure too many feel to raise test scores. Expensive SAT prep courses have been available for decades to those who can afford them (and learning test-taking strategies works, or they wouldn't be so popular). But taking tests and reading are not the same thing.

9. Tests that don't measure what we know is important waste time that could otherwise have been spent learning. I include the time teachers spend analyzing and interpreting meaningless scores instead of engaging in professional development to improve the teaching of reading.

10. Until we can accurately measure the growth of individual students over the time they spend with a teacher, we can't use test scores to tell us anything about a teacher's skill. If my students aren't remarkably better readers and writers in June, I should lose my job. But unless we know where they're starting from in September and what I'm teaching, we can't begin to understand the significance of their gains in June.

Here is a brief overview of assessment I would support:

1. A student's reading list and his or her reflections, in writing, on the growth and challenges in reading over the school year, along with a videotape of the student reading aloud and discussing a text.

2. A portfolio of samples of a student's reading across genres and increasingly complex texts and samples of writing demonstrating skill and understanding.

3. Principals reviewing assessment products with a teacher. English departments discussing assessment results and designing pedagogy that elicits students' understanding. Professional development targeted to helping us improve our practices.

4. Plans and suggestions for each student passed on to next year's teacher, plus time before the start of the school year to get to know incoming students through their reading and writing portfolios. Imagine starting the school year analyzing students' reading lists, reflections, and writing portfolios.

I only wish I believed that assessment that makes sense might happen in the years left in my career. Since I can't count on it in my school or district, my work in my classroom focuses on thinking deeply about individual students and understanding what they need to improve.

Schoolwide Reading Break

If reading—by extensive exposure and intensive interaction—cannot be made enjoyable and easy, there is no hope for students in their later education.

—*Helen Vendler*

I am blessed to have a principal who used to own a bookstore. He has other good qualities, like his genuine affection for teenagers and his deep commitment to education, but he also has a passion for reading that has propelled our school forward. Neal found his zeal for reading long after he finished his schooling—when he bought a bookstore and realized he couldn't sell what he didn't read—and now he can't go a day without it. He understands the years wasted, especially by adolescents, *not* reading books.

Even as our budget has been squeezed and scrutinized each year, Neal has continued to carve out funds for books. I believe this commitment originated in two places: his personal love of reading and watching my 2009 video about students from our high school who fake their way through English class. (It is available on the Heinemann website.) Neal was inspired by the turnaround my nonreaders made in just one semester and the volume of reading seniors were doing. He knew that classrooms in which this is standard practice help students but that a whole-school effort would change our culture and create a lasting impact not only on individual students but our entire community. We soon had evidence of Neal's commitment: he tripled our school library budget and committed a thousand dollars per English teacher for classroom libraries. Impressive, yes, but he did something truly revolutionary when he then supported our whole-school reading break initiative.

A committee of teachers began studying the idea of a reading break in the spring of 2010. We read the 2007 report from the National Endowment of the Arts, "To Read or Not to Read: A Question of National Importance," and took to heart this summary statement:

> As Americans, especially younger Americans, read less, they read less well. Because they read less well, they have lower levels of academic achievement. (The shameful fact that nearly one third of American teenagers drop out of school is deeply connected to declining literacy and reading comprehension.) With lower levels of reading and writing ability, people do less well in the job market. Poor reading skills correlate heavily with lack of employment, lower wages, and fewer opportunities for advancement. (5)

It reads like a description of our valley in the mountains of New Hampshire.

To understand my school, you need to understand a little of its history. Six years ago our high school had the highest dropout rate in the state. Our school had run through several principals over a short period of time, leaving students and programs in chaos and prompting teachers to seek more stable working conditions elsewhere. Forty percent of our high school teachers left over three years. The seams of our school unraveled. We hired five new English teachers each year for three years and watched all of them leave each spring. Too many of our families were juggling several part-time jobs to heat their homes each winter, sacrificing time with their children, and our school lacked a deep commitment to improving literacy. Our curriculum was a mess. We knew our graduates were struggling to pay for college programs that met their aspirations and struggling to meet academic expectations once they got there, but individual teachers felt powerless to improve things.

We turned this around.

It began with a principal, Jack Loynd, who had an unwavering, laser-focused commitment to improvement. He believed in teachers and for nine years helped us change course. The dropout spike happened during his watch because the factors that led us there were remarkably challenging to overcome. But he stayed focused, the district built a new high school, and last year only one student dropped out in a student population near 900. He is now a math teacher at our school, still leading students and teachers to excellence. He is brilliant, self-sacrificing, and humble and has been one of the most important influences on my professional life.

Even with our turnaround gaining steam, we knew our students were not reading enough. We surveyed students and staff to gather evidence. We focused on whole books because even our strongest students were sort of reading online like most adolescents but not consistently reading their assignments in English class and the content areas. Once we looked, we realized the problem was bigger than we imagined. About 20 percent of our students said they read books regularly, about 30 percent read a book or two a year, and the remaining 50 percent said they did not read books at all. We found dozens of students who had *never* read a chapter book. Not one. Not in late elementary school, not in middle school, and certainly not now in high school.

A kid who doesn't read in high school will be unlikely to read as a young adult. As the NEA report found, "Nearly half of all Americans ages 18 to 24 read no books for pleasure" (2007, 7). Or as Richard Allington (2001) has said, "We seem to be producing readers who can read more difficult texts but readers who elect not to read even easy texts on their own time" (8).

The reading break committee proposed sustained silent reading for the whole school for twenty minutes a day. Groups of between ten and twelve students comprising all grade levels, 9–12, would be assigned to teachers and staff members in areas throughout the school (we investigated every possible space in which students could gather in order to keep the groups small). The break would include ten minutes for student-produced video announcements at the start or end, thus requiring a total of thirty minutes. We discussed our proposal with department chairs, fielded and investigated questions and challenges, and then presented it to the faculty. We were cautiously skeptical, but the reading break received strong support from the teachers and became part of the daily schedule two years ago.

Four mornings a week at 9:00 A.M. Kennett High School becomes nearly silent. Between first and second block, students gather in classrooms, conference rooms, the weight room, corners of the auditorium, science labs, and even the faculty lounge to read with teachers. And it works. Kids read. Their academic performance is improving. We should expect good results when we increase time to read in school. Allington continues, "The analyses [between direct reading and reading growth] suggest that an increase of five minutes daily silent reading would be predicted to produce an additional month's growth on a standardized reading achievement test" (31). We believe we will create passionate, voracious readers with increased access to terrific books and time to read.

As you can imagine, there were a few obstacles beyond the usual stumbles of any September. Here is how we worked around them.

Providing access to books. It isn't enough to have a well-stocked school library; teachers must have books in their classrooms. Some days students leave books behind in cars or lockers, and teachers need to be able to put reading in the hands of these students. We sent out a request for donations to our community and filled bins around the school. Our media specialist provided back copies of a wide range of magazines. We have newspapers delivered and books on carts for teachers who oversee reading break in places where books can't remain permanently. Every space has books available at a variety of ability levels.

Dealing with students who don't want to read books. We allow newspapers and magazines as a way into reading for resistant students, but our goal is to get every student into a book because we believe in the sustained engagement with thinking that books provide. We also believe that reading books improves confidence. As one of my students wrote in his notebook, "I beat my reading goal by 50+ pages this week. That's what I'm talking about. I have never read a decently long book in less than one week. I feel a sense of pride and I feel more responsible and grown up. I don't know why, but it's weird." We know most of our students already spend plenty of time online, so we don't allow connecting to the Internet during reading break. Our students don't need additional practice in skimming headlines and clicking between web pages.

Maintaining silence. Outside of school 58 percent of middle and high school students report that they use other media while reading (NEA 2007), so students aren't allowed to wear headphones during reading break. Distractions affect comprehension. Our goal is to develop the capacity for sustained, focused attention. As Nicholas Carr says:

> The reading of a sequence of printed pages was valuable not just for the knowledge readers acquired from the author's words but for the way those words set off intellectual vibrations within their own minds. In the quiet spaces opened up by the prolonged, undistracted reading of a book, people made their own associations, drew their own inferences and analogies, fostered their own ideas. They thought deeply as they read deeply. Even the earliest silent readers recognized the striking change in their consciousness that took place as they immersed them- selves in the pages of a book. The medieval bishop Isaac of Syria described how, whenever he read to himself, "as in a dream, I enter a state when my sense and thoughts are concentrated. Then, when with prolonging of this silence the turmoil of memories is stilled in my heart, ceaseless waves of joy are sent me by inner thoughts, beyond expecta- tion suddenly arising to delight my heart." Reading a book was a meditative act, but it didn't involve a clearing of the mind. It involved a filling, or replenishing, of the mind. Readers disengaged their attention from the outward flow of passing stimuli in order to engage it more deeply with an inward flow of words, ideas, and emotions. (2010, 65)

I'm not implying that creating twenty minutes of silence in a high school each day is easy, only that we value it and work for it.

Establishing clear, consistent expectations. Ours were created with input from our faculty. Some teachers do not comply, however. Ever notice how similar rebel teachers can be to rebel students? High school kids are quick to talk, so yes, we hear rumors of teachers who allow students to complete homework or sleep during reading break. We follow up on it. We have a team of floating administrators and guidance coun- selors who are not assigned a group of students but rotate through classrooms and reading areas each day. Any area might have a visitor at any time. It all comes down to commitment and belief. Teachers who understand that literacy changes lives work to make reading break a positive but focused time for all kids. Teachers who believe reading is a waste of time don't work very hard to uphold high expectations. Teachers who have a fixed-performance view of intelligence don't believe kids will improve as readers given time to read, so they don't expect much from reading break. Those who want to help kids develop a dynamic view of their own intelligence keep trying.

Recommending books. Most of our teachers have no idea what to recommend to teenagers who don't want to read. We have book lists and televised book trailers created by students; we send our media specialist to classrooms with stacks of good reading. We invite kids and teachers to browse the new releases in the library. Emails zip around the building asking for suggestions to match a kid's interests. My colleague Cindy Davis created a wall of book covers and had kids sign under the ones they had read. This generated a lot of interest.

Dealing with nonreaders. First, we ask teachers to *invite* kids into reading, not force them into it. We want suggestions and encouragement and a commitment to helping students find a good fit book. This is job one: modeling enjoyment, passion, and the value of reading. We have small groups, so it's possible.

When students say they hate reading, we say, "Then you haven't found the right book yet, one that will keep you reading." And we make a commitment to seek out that book for a kid who has never found one. We listen, match books to interests and ability, and keep trying.

If all the suggestions and encouragement don't work or a student is defiant, the student is placed in a reading group in which students share a common text and read out loud together. These small groups are run by administers and guidance counselors; they are not punishment—they are powerful.

My principal, Neal, started the Man Group our first year. We had a crew of frequently disruptive and suspended boys who had been kicked out of reading break for noncompliance. Each one had a history of struggle with school and reading in particular. Neal invited these eight boys to his office, and reading break took on new importance. He used this daily time to mentor and encourage them but mostly to share his love of reading. He began by ordering nine copies of a book he loved, *Alabama Moon*, so that each boy could follow along as he read aloud. He also led discussions about the reading, listening to the boys and encouraging their understanding and connections to the story.

Here's when we knew it had changed them: if suspended, the boys would stop by for a copy of the book so they could keep up with the reading. They carried the book in the halls. When I interviewed them just a few months into their new assignments, the boys spoke positively about reading break and the book.

The Man Group read *Alabama Moon*, *Dirt Road Home*, *POP*, *Hole in My Life*, and *Deadline* that year. They showed up on time; they volunteered to read aloud in the group; they were utterly unlike the boys I interviewed when they were thrown out of class. When they finished a book they would record a group book talk to be broadcast as part of our televised morning announcements. They filmed their interviews in shirts and ties. My principal loved the opportunity to mentor these young men in reading. One boy, a word-by-word reader as a senior, learned to read in phrases during his time in the group. He changed from a kid who told me, "Reading has always been hard for me," to one who told me he would read to his own children some day.

I interviewed many students about the experience of reading break at the end of our first year. Jordan said:

> I think reading reduces stress, at least for the time in which you're
> reading. I'm always excited to go to reading break because that means
> I can just stop thinking about everything and only concentrate on my
> book. I can zone everything else out and be fully absorbed in my book.
> It makes me feel better after. It was like finally taking a breath for the
> day. Reading cleanses me. I think reading break is great; I just wish there
> was a way to have it on Thursdays as well because I hate not having
> that breathing time. [*Thursdays have a delayed start to accommodate our
> professional learning communities.*]

Jordan read six books the year before reading break was introduced and fourteen when given this regular time to read.

We expected naysayers and had them—the acerbic columnist who complained in our local paper that reading in school was just a way for teachers to be lazy, and the math teacher who wanted to know when the whole school would be practicing his content area for twenty minutes a day. But we also had tremendous support. Parents called to thank us, donated books, even came in to recommend one to a class. Many students, although initially resistant, confessed that it was the first reading they had done (and eventually enjoyed) in years.

This was all predictable. Here's what surprised me: teachers.

I live in a bubble of reading delight. I have books piled on almost every surface of my house. I know there are adults who don't like reading, but I figured college-educated folks were rarely among them. And as naïve as this sounds, I believed teachers were far more likely to be readers than anyone else. I simply couldn't continue to grow as a teacher if I weren't reading.

And then I walked into a math teacher's reading break one day in April. He said to his class, "I want you all to know before this school year, the last time I read a book was before any of you were born." He told students he had never liked reading but that this year he had the time so he read six books, one of more than seven hundred pages. He said he couldn't believe all he had been missing. I was grateful for his honesty but stunned by his admission. I wondered how rare he was.

It turns out, not at all. Jim Trelease, author of *The Read-Aloud Handbook* (2006), reports:

> One study of 224 teachers pursuing graduate degrees showed they read few or no professional journals that included research. More than half said they had read only one or two professional books in the previous year, and an additional 20 percent said they had read nothing in the last six months or one year. *This means that teachers don't read any more often than adults in the general population (where the majority don't have a degree beyond high school).*
>
> More recently, in a 1998 national survey of 666 academic high school teachers, almost half reported not reading one professional journal or magazine. The 51 percent who did such reading regularly were also more apt to belong to professional associations linked to their teaching area. The survey group averaged fifteen years of teaching, with 63 percent holding graduate degrees. (100–101)

What an indictment.

One teacher confessed he had never read—not even in college. He said his life was plenty meaningful without reading. He just didn't buy its value. He was persuasive and determined as he challenged me that spring, but he also believed that consistency matters in a school and if everyone was going to read at 9:00 each day, he would, too. And he did. He read for his graduate courses, he read for his content area, and finally, he began reading mysteries for pleasure. In that one school year, he found what had slipped by him for twenty-five years: reading is a rewarding and fascinating mind journey. Imagine the impact his realization will have on the way he interacts with his students in the dozens of years left in his career.

All of this reminds me of shopping for a refrigerator. Pat and I have been on the hunt for a new one this month. Ours leaks. Each time we open one in a showroom its emptiness jolts me, all those shelves of nothingness. Sometimes the sellers have anticipated this and there is colored-cardboard pretend food in clean drawers to help us see this fridge in our own kitchen. But pretend is pretend. From the outside these refrigerators all *look* whole, but they remind me of Jason, who I observed during reading break last week. He had *Gym Candy* propped open on his desk while he played with a keychain hanging off his binder. He signed out to the bathroom and returned reluctantly to his seat a few minutes later. He slyly turned the page of the novel every few minutes until the end of the period. Not reading can be a slick performance.

I walked him to his next class. We talked about reading and he was quick to be honest, as most kids are. He's never read a book—not one. He's a sophomore so he's been read to—he's been told about a lot of books—he's been quizzed on what they mean, given study guides and handouts—but all that work has not required him to read. He's a showroom refrigerator with colored-cardboard pretend reading experiences lining the shelves inside. And unless we do something differently, he doesn't stand a chance in this world of increasing literacy demands. Nonreaders are sidelined into low-paying jobs with little advancement every time.

I know how this happens. Kids slip by us. There are so many of them and there is so little time each day, with so much to teach. We all have content expectations and common assessments and discipline reports and phone calls to make, and suddenly the individual reading habits of a hundred (or more) kids seems impossible to monitor or remedy. One thing reading break has given our school is a way to notice. I regularly get reports about nonreaders, but I don't get discouraged. I am relieved that our school is finally noticing and advocating for these individual kids.

If you stop by Kennett this week you'll find hundreds of students with books tucked in backpacks and coat pockets. Kennett students expect to read every day. You'll find more talk about books than we've ever experienced at our school before. You'll see teachers' current reading lists posted in their classrooms and student-designed Kennett Reads posters in unlikely places (see three of these in the photos at the beginning of this chapter). We are committed to developing a community of readers. I believe it all happened because we hired the principal who used to own a bookstore. See what I mean about the power of reading?

Summer Reading

*Rest is not idleness, and to lie sometimes on the grass on a summer day
listening to the murmur of water, or watching the clouds float across the sky,
is hardly a waste of time.*

—*John Lubbock*

It's summertime and I'm in my chair by the window, looking out at the backyard. I've just taken my dogs out for a walk in the cool, still morning and looked up at the pale blue sky amidst all this green. I love July. Love it. There is something wonderful about living in the mountains. I embrace the trees and the silence and the green that surrounds me, out every window.

Today I'm scribbling about the Brontës when I look up into the face of a black bear. His head almost fills the open window beside me as he plods down the granite steps into the back yard. The sound of his footsteps and his breathing have my heart beating fast. Then, shaking my head in wonder, I see a second one pass by my window.

Summer is something, that's for sure.

If school is the buckle-down-get-those-assignments-done rhythm September to June, then summer is everything but that. In fact, summer is life *after* school. Students' relationship with reading during the summer is a pretty good window into what that relationship will be once they leave our classrooms for good. We have an opportunity with summer reading to open that window to individual passions and interests and at the same time prevent the loss of achievement that months without practice bring.

We need kids to read in the summer. And sure, they'll skim-read on the computer. Some people say we should count that as reading; in fact, parents who credit online reading as reading tell me their kids read all the time. But this is shallow reading. It's not the same as sinking into a book for pages and pages. It doesn't develop the skills that make doing so possible. If anything, students are practicing a *lack* of attention and deep thinking. We're kidding ourselves about what most kids read online anyway: Gui read Craigslist ads, Zach searched for upgrades for his Jeep; J. P. checked box scores. All three were quite honest about their online reading—no newspapers, no articles, no blogs, nothing that required more than a glancing interest. They were accomplished fake readers in English class. College-prep seniors who don't read: you know how that story will end.

Our remedy to the summer reading slump is to assign books. It's a necessity. Students need to practice the deep concentration and stamina book reading requires. But we've had some problems getting students to actually read them. Why? Let me answer with a story about my own son.

In the summer after Cameron's freshman year in high school I was an anxious parent. He was my first child and like most parents, I believed he was the best at everything. Had there ever been a child this wonderful? Cam had a natural love of learning, always, but once he entered high school, he became lethargic and hostile about most things school. I knew what was ahead and I worried. Somehow I wanted to counteract what was happening in high school with rich experiences in learning, especially in the summer when I had him with me for longer stretches of time.

Cam turned fifteen in March of his freshman year. Fifteen is hard. For many kids, the light for living dims this year. Cam spent most of that year in his hooded hockey sweatshirt, slouched and brooding as his burst of height stretched him rail thin and made him less graceful, less sure. He wore glasses instead of contacts and grew his hair long in curls that framed a permanent scowl. It was the end of playfulness and he just wasn't ready. I remember a long ride home that winter from a hockey tournament in the southwest corner of our state. Our conversation was easy because you can say anything in the cave of the front seat with no eye contact, surrounded by pitch black and out of the range of good radio.

Cam lamented, "In seventh grade we all talked about kissing girls, now they all talk about is sleeping with them." I kept my eyes on the road. Cam saw his entire world shifting. He was always a gifted, natural athlete, but he was beginning to see that window closing as he encountered hockey players in Canada and watched the kids he most admired from our varsity team choose a Division III team to play for in college, realizing his best wasn't going to take him to the NHL.

And school? He didn't understand why it had to be so dull. He could do the work, but it was pointless to him. His grades slipped to Bs and he blamed his teachers. Summer reading at our house in those weeks between Cam's freshman and sophomore years had two parts: *Harry Potter and the Order of the Phoenix* and *The Tale of Two Cities*.

Imagine the four of us—Pat, Cam, Hannah, and I—each night after dinner stretched across the living room listening as one of us read aloud. Each book in the series was parceled out a chapter a night. (Sometimes three or more when we just couldn't stop.) Imagine all those natural conversations that followed—"I couldn't believe it!" "Do you think—?" "What if—?" We took *Harry Potter and Half-Blood Prince* with us to Ireland and read it in one amazing setting after another, including one night's stay in a castle near Dublin that had its own ghost. We stood in London on the night *Harry Potter and the Deathly Hollows* was released—along with five thousand Brits chanting, "We want Harry!"—and then read many chapters a night during our stay, finishing before we returned to New Hampshire. (Yeah, we even plan vacations around books at my house.)

Now return to that couch in our living room on an August Saturday night. Pat and I come home from playing cards with friends to find Cam waiting, Dickens in hand. "Mom," he says before we've even shut the door, "tell me I don't have to read this book!"

I cringe. I love *The Tale of Two Cities*. I recommended it. My department has given students a list of five or six titles to choose from, and since Cam is taking honors English in the fall I feel he should read something challenging. And I've fallen into that mistaken belief about summer—that he'll have all that time, so even if it's hard, he can do it. Now here it is August and he's barely started.

"Look at this"—he places his hand to mark a page—"from here, all the way"—flip, flip, flip—"to *here* is all about a hat!" I sigh. I start to give him my defense of the book and stop. I remember reading it for the first time—the thrill of that story. I was on vacation during my third year of teaching, far past high school. I had endurance and a willingness to read simply because I was well beyond the awkward adolescent I had been at fifteen.

This is one of the things I mean by a mismatch between text and student. Cam *could* have read the book that summer (and would have, he was always compliant), but the intricacies of the French Revolution and the true beauty of the sacrifice a man might make for his friend would likely have slipped past him. I don't believe we can call it rigorous reading when a student is simply reading to get it over with and is so distant from the heart of the story that if it is remembered at all, it will be remembered with distaste. It is, I believe, what Louise Rosenblatt (1976) meant when she said:

> Those who cram the classics down students' throats long before they are ready are careless of the fate of the great works of the past. Even though the majority were to graduate from school and high school without having encountered many of the great authors, we should not need to be alarmed if they had the ability to read with understanding and had acquired zest for the experience that literature can give. Those who try to crowd into the school years everything that "ought" to be read evidently assume that the youth will never read again after school years are over. . . . [T]o force such works on the young prematurely defeats the long-term goal of educating people to a personal love of literature sufficiently deep to cause them to seek it out for themselves at the appropriate time. (217)

Thankfully I had a choice that summer. We went back to the department list and Cam chose *Eleven Seconds*, by Travis Roy, the story of a Boston University hockey player who was paralyzed after eleven seconds on the ice as a freshman. Cam read with energy, ready to talk and think and share his wonder at Roy's resiliency with my husband and me night after night.

Summer is not the time to toss in the books we can't get to during the year but think kids should read or the books we think will make our school look more impressive if we require them. It's not the time to make students who want to take honors English "earn" it. Summer means they're on their own. Summer reading in most schools is absent instruction or discussion. Many students won't have parents reading beside them, ready to talk. We need books that can and will be read independently.

We should take misery more seriously. What we feel as we learn matters. It isn't fun I'm advocating here, but pleasure. Pleasure from the hard work of staying with a book for hours. We have to recognize that misery doesn't promote learning and often prevents retention. It leads to disengagement and mistrust, not just in us, but in reading as something worthy of our time. As Alicia said to me after four years of honors courses, "I thought all books were boring, so I didn't read them. Even the SparkNotes were boring."

How can we interest kids in summer reading? We must answer this question because the summer reading gap is real. Students who don't read all summer return to school in the fall behind kids who read. Richard Allington, speaking at the Colorado Council of the International Reading Association's conference in Denver in February of 2012, shared the following: "Struggling readers from any income level experience summer reading setback. Summer reading loss results in a three-year gap in achievement by the end of third grade. Every two and a quarter years, low-income students who don't read in the summer fall a year behind."

Solutions are obvious. Keep our school libraries open through June, July, and August, even into the evening. Staff them with people who love books and can't stop talking about them and will put them in the hands of kids. Set up book clubs to bring readers together. Send bookmobiles to the homes of kids who can't make it to school. Send free books to good homes all over town in imitation of the Portland, Oregon, bike program (which lets you pick one up and ride as far as you need it, then leave it for someone else)—pick up a book somewhere and return it somewhere else with a recommendation on the inside cover. Sponsor author events in town and read-alouds for all ages. Make reading engagement job one for your entire community. Recognize the many reading authorities you have in town—like George in ours, who owns a successful local business and knows so many great history books. Celebrate and share those individual passions.

What a wonderful world it would be.

I don't live in that world, so let me tell you what worked at my school.

One year we copied book covers onto chart paper with space below for kids to sign up if they were interested in reading the book with a teacher. (Teachers chose books they wanted to read with kids in addition to required texts for honors and AP courses.) The deal? Agree to read the book and attend a one-hour book discussion and you were freed from the back-to-school summer reading assignment, which requires everyone to write a letter about their summer reading and turn it in for a grade on the first day of school. (Naturally, many kids start the year with a zero. I still hate this practice.)

I thought I was a little crazy when I first asked the department chairs to consider this alternative to summer reading. I figured a few colleagues and I would have reading groups, but instead, the energy was contagious. One teacher chose a former President's biography; another chose a popular mystery; one English teacher put the entire Twilight series on her chart, which filled up in record time and prompted pleas from dozens to "Let me read with you, Ms. Tilton!" Teachers posted book invitations on their classroom doors or in the hallway leading to the cafeteria.

I ran three groups, two on required reading for senior economics, and one on *The Book Thief*. I remember sitting with a dozen kids in the gazebo on a hill near the school and discussing *Nickel & Dimed*. The kids brought their notes and their thinking about the hardscrabble life of the working poor and pointed out how the jobs the author of the book took reminded them of the employment opportunities in our valley. It was the small class we all dream of, with time to let every kid talk on a perfect July afternoon. Carrie took her group, who read a biography of firefighters killed in Montana, to the Jackson Firehouse. Our assistant principal met with three groups of freshmen to talk about *Under the Persimmon Tree*. My husband, a small-business owner, and his friend, a Realtor, agreed to meet with a group of students to give the businessman's view of *Nickel & Dimed*.

We didn't get all students to sign up, of course. But in our first year we had fifty-four reading groups, and more than half the student body participated. Every one of the groups had great energy. A group of girls blogged excitedly about the plot twists in the Twilight series. The AP U.S. history teacher extended his book club throughout the fall, meeting each Wednesday night at a local coffee house. (Those kids had read eight books with him by the time they disbanded.) Another teacher chose *Why Good Things Happen to Good People* and the twelve students he met with became so committed to the ideas in the book, they organized fundraisers to create a thousand-dollar scholarship for a senior headed to college. As with most things that involve education, kids and teachers exceed our expectations when we let them loose to lead.

Summer reading should invoke pleasure—relaxation—opportunity. Challenge kids to read three books by one author so they can speculate on a writer's growth or read three books from a similar time period or analyze the prejudices and unspoken values in a series of fantasy novels. Let students set their own goals for summer reading and I guarantee some will choose and make time for the classics and read more than we'd ever assign to them. (Probably about the same percentage as will eventually major in English—currently under two—but I've learned that most others *will* read as well if we guide them.)

Asking Hard Questions

It's all well and good to transform our classrooms. It's very good, in fact; it just might keep us there for many more years. Looking back over the years I've spent teaching, I'm grateful. What a gift this work and these students and colleagues have been in my life.

But one classroom of readers in a school is not enough. It may be where we need to start, but when we're ready, we have to talk with our colleagues. I'm not guaranteeing they'll listen, only suggesting that we need to think together about ways we can reach more readers. We're all in this together, and the truth is, transforming a school culture has the power to truly change our community and our world.

I don't like this part of being a professional. I've never been a fan of confrontation. I like everyone to be happy. I bake cookies and keep a bowl of candy in my office. I organize meals when someone is ill. I'd rather comfort the kid who just got snapped at by the impatient lunch lady than confront the lunch lady on her unnecessary cruelty. Confrontation means the minefield of a long conversation. It is so much easier to walk back to class promising myself to be nicer to my students to make up for all the barbs they might absorb during a school day.

I avoid the people who like to complain about how unappreciated we are as teachers and how everyone expects miracles but gives us too many kids and too few books. To me it is like putting on one of those chain-mail suits knights used to wear in battle; it's all too much to carry. What gives me energy? What makes me want to work harder? Asking questions of myself and my teaching and then trying to answer them. It's the hard work I believe we must do in order to move our profession forward. It's the hard work we must do in order to help students realize their aspirations for college. But that doesn't make it any less hard.

I ran into a moment like this last week when a former colleague got upset about an interview I'd videotaped with a student who said he did not read in middle school the year before. "I know what you're doing here, and I'm telling you you're asking the wrong questions," he nearly shouted at me. "Reading doesn't matter. What you should have asked him—have you eaten today? will you be sleeping at home tonight? Reading means nothing to him."

And I almost agree—but I don't.

I know about the kids who have little because I was one during a few dark years in my childhood. Food mattered. Hand-me-downs mattered. My dad's drinking mattered. But I also know that reading saved me. *Reading* saved me because I escaped into the world of *The Great Brain* and imagined a different life. And maybe all I'm doing is saving myself again and again when I track down one book for Adam tonight, ordering it and paying for it myself, on the chance that he *will* read. On the chance that it might be pleasurable and meaningful and it might show him light in an otherwise dark life, which includes his father's current incarceration. And maybe that *doesn't* matter. Maybe my colleague is right and all my efforts for this kid this year will fail. That will hurt. But doing nothing would hurt more. I'm not giving up on the healing power of story. And I'm not giving up on facing the truth about practices that distance kids from books instead of pulling them near. Because reading matters. It is foolish to think otherwise.

We can't wait for someone else to teach our students to love books. *We* are the miracle workers. Teaching is still about hope and when we lose sight of that, the minute we say, "I can't," or "That kid won't," we should walk away—leave the school and start walking. Here in my town I could be in the woods in a minute on a golden carpet of leaves. It's cold in the shadow of the trees, but I'll warm up. I could ascend Mt. Chocorua and be stunned by the view at the top. Breathe it all in and remember why I'm here and the opportunity that lies in my hands. These kids. This day. Reading might show a girl how to lose her best friend and her mother and still, somehow, stand upright with dignity and honor (*Please Ignore Vera Deitz*). Or reading might tell a young man there are kids out there like him and there *will* be joy ahead (*The Curious Incident of the Dog in the Night-Time*). Reading might help a son understand what his father faced in Vietnam (*Fallen Angels*) or a brother understand the nightmares of his older sister, who is home on leave from Iraq (*What a Brother Knows*). I could keep going on for pages.

Ignore the ranting social studies teacher in the corner who says, and I quote a teacher at my workshop today, "What good is reading some throwaway novel like *Boot Camp* when he sees the biology textbook at college this fall?" Ignore him, but not for the reason you think. I know *Boot Camp* is not challenging enough to prepare a senior for college reading, but this is a teacher who told me about his seventh graders, "They are reluctant readers, so I tell them they can read the textbook if they want to, but I'll go over it all in class." Doing nothing to prepare readers is worse.

When a student who's never read chooses *Boot Camp*, I let him, but I worry. I work to move him into more challenging books during the year, but if you think starting with only challenging books is the answer, then why didn't it work in seventh, eighth, ninth, tenth, or eleventh grade with this boy? As I said to the social studies teacher, "Kids need to build fluency and stamina. That matters. *Boot Camp* is helping him do that, so it is important work for him to do now. What we need to do is increase the complexity of the texts he's reading over time, as he buys into his own development in reading. And we have to teach him how to read increasingly complex texts in every class in the school, including yours."

I'd like you to eavesdrop on a conversation I had with a woman in Michigan a week ago. She told me she was trying to promote more reading in her classes after reading Kelly Gallagher's *Readicide*. I smiled. Yes, I loved that book and Kelly's courage in writing it. But how many of us read it, set it aside, and went back to what we were doing before? She said, "We only teach a few class novels now, and I know some don't read them, but we have to teach them, and if some only read a chapter," she hesitated, tucking her hair behind her ear again and glancing around the bar, "at least they had an experience with that book and know something about it. Right?" She looked at me.

"Are you asking whether that's a good trade for the time spent on it?" I know as I ask the question that she's already answered it. That's where her anxiety is coming from. She looks guilty. I don't want her to feel bad, but I want her to ask herself these hard questions and struggle to answer them. I want us to struggle together. Because we don't feel the power of this work when we do what we *have* to do, especially when we recognize it is not helping the students we so want to help. "So you have to teach the book, and you say you recognize that the kids who won't read might read one chapter over four weeks—"

"Five or six," she corrects me. We both flinch.

"So you recognize that one chapter of reading in six weeks is not enough reading for this reluctant, struggling, whatever-you-call-him reader, but it's the best you can get out of him because the book is beyond his ability to read independently based mostly on its slow pace and the uninteresting content for most fourteen-year-old boys—in other words, you recognize that these six weeks might have failed to help this boy improve as a reader. You're trying to justify it. You hope he has a connection to our country's literature history. And you're hoping that matters enough." I look at her with sympathy. "I know what this is like. I've been there and it hurts even to ask the question. I'm watching ninth graders caught in this same swirl right now in my school. What we know we need to change can feel too hard."

She winces, but she's listening. We're having this conversation because we already have a relationship and we're at a conference together, both of us here because we want to be better teachers, and over a glass of wine sometimes I say what I'm really thinking. Don't imagine I find it easy to do this in my own school, though. I've tried, but sometimes I get tired of repeating myself and not being heard. These are conversations we should have with our colleagues, wherever we find them.

Kids who aren't reading are not engaged in learning that lasts. The few things they tell us about the book are not coming from discovery and thinking—which is what learning requires. They're reciting what they've been told. What do they remember years or months or even weeks later? "Yeah, not a good book. Boring," as a twelfth grader told me about *To Kill a Mockingbird* this fall when I asked him.

Here's a thought: no kid should pass English any year without reading dozens of books. Not how many hard books did we drag them through, but how many hours they spent reading. And it's remarkably hard to pull off. But the question to ask is *how* can we do it? What does it look like when we know it is happening for most students in the room? How can we tap into the individual thinking that is happening for kids when they encounter all these different books?

I do not need to answer these questions for you. You don't need an "expert" to come in and tell you how to make it happen. We are smart enough to solve this problem in our own school if we ask the questions that nag at us and then work together to solve problems. I need to ask as a fellow professional that you answer them for your students and for yourself. I want you to confront what feels impossible and at every juncture simply ask, "How can we solve that problem?" Because when I do that I empower you to use all of your intellect to find an answer to a question that matters.

And you might say, "*To Kill a Mockingbird* matters."

I'd say, "Only if they are reading it."

Let's start there and see what we can figure out together.

Your Reading Life Matters

Last year I read 140 books (the titles are posted on Paul Hankins' Facebook site, "The Centurions of 2011") and I'm feeling pretty guilty about that. I use reading to avoid doing harder things like writing this book or cooking dinner. You could divide up my reading list into four parts: young adult literature I will recommend in class; mindless, easy reading I use to fill time on planes or when I'm stressed; classic and modern literature that feeds me; and professional books. Here are titles from this month for three of the categories: *How It Ends*, by Laura Weiss (young adult literature), *Salvage the Bones*, by Jesmyn Ward (modern literature that feeds me), and *Sit Down and Teach Up*, by Katie Wood Ray and Matt Glover (professional books). I have three titles on my nightstand at the moment: *Last Night at Twisted River*, by John Irving, *The Wild Things*, by Dave Eggers, and *Old Friend from Far Away*, by Natalie Goldberg. (I'm going to keep the mindless, easy reading books to myself. Some of these are so bad I leave them behind at airport gates, pretending I've never seen them before.)

I have a large stack of books I wanted to read this summer and haven't gotten to yet and a page in my notebook (just like the one I ask my students to keep) that lists titles others have recommended that I'm determined to get to. Sometimes I order a large number of these all at once and then slowly read my way through them. That's how I found *Let the Great World Spin*, purchased months ago and one among many on my desk until I picked it up one morning and was swept away, devouring the entire thing by evening. The writing is rich, the story so compelling, the experience of reading it so satisfying, that I fear I'll never find a book as good again. And I said that last month at the end of *The Well and the Mine*.

We live in a great time for readers. Hundreds of thousands of books are published each year in our country alone, according to an index that measures the standard of living. The total number published in America has dropped by 18 percent since 2006, but in that same time, self-published books grew to forty thousand a month. I love that I will never truly be an authority on the best books for students or middle-aged female readers like myself. I know the well is deep and book love will regenerate itself continually in my life. I bring that assurance and that passion into my room each day. It matters. I mention it because I've had English teachers tell me they don't like reading. Or they don't like young adult literature—after which they usually mention that they haven't really read any, just a few that were inferior to the titles they believe are important to know. You're choking on your toast, aren't you? You can't believe anyone would teach English and not love books. As Jim Trelease (2006) says, "You can't catch a cold or a love of books from someone who has neither" (101).

Reading teachers read.

But if I tell you some English teachers have said they don't write, you'll nod and keep reading. And I will say we can't teach something we don't practice. We can't. We don't do it well. If you want to teach readers, you're going to have to read some of the books that students say are fabulous but you've resisted because they're unfamiliar. I've listed some of my favorites on my website but you can also poke around on Goodreads or the American Library Association or other places dedicated to readers and find reviews, summaries, and passages to entice you to read. Follow big readers on twitter for frequent updates (@donalynbooks, @PaulWHankins, @ColbySharp, @frankiSibberson or @MrSchuReads) or log on to #titletalk on the last Sunday of each month.

I force myself to know books I wouldn't choose, so that I can recommend them to my diverse readers. I sample biographies and war books, fantasy and science fiction. I depend on students' book talks for information on the many books I can't get to. As Jasper said to me one afternoon, "Mrs. Kittle, you've never booktalked a book I would read. You and I don't like the same kinds of books." Jasper read faithfully, ravenously, almost all fantasy. I confess those books aren't for me, but I can't just tolerate his choices, I must guide him toward challenge and depth, so I have to learn more about them. Jasper was a patient teacher, and I'm better at my work because of him.

We keep lists to celebrate our reading, to wonder about our reading, to advertise our reading to others who might benefit from our choices, and to consider next books for the diversity of readers in our classrooms. What are the next books for someone who loved *Red Kayak*, by Priscilla Cummings? I need to have an answer to that. I will find it by reading.

Start Where They Are

~*~*~

*Being swept away by a combination of great story and great writing—
of being flattened, in fact—is part of every writer's necessary formation.
You cannot hope to sweep someone else away by the force of your writing
until it has been done to you.*

—Stephen King

I stubbornly continue to believe I can do anything. That it probably can't be done is a motivator to me, always has been. Some kids refuse my help. Some drop out. I hate this part of teaching. But miracles teach me possibility. The miracles keep me in the classroom. The Hail Mary pass with time running out—that's the one I caught with Crystal.

Crystal was in my general-level English class her senior year, a course for the most struggling students in the school. I believe it is educational malpractice to continue to lump kids into classes built more on behavior than ability. Students believe they are in those courses because they're dumb. It is one of the tragedies of the school system for me: the bottom-level track, the students who have been defiant, or as Crystal explained, "who shut down and stop doing work" when frustrated, the ones who are willing to fail, those kids think the levels in high school courses correspond to intelligence. They think they're not good enough for college prep or honors.

"General level" signals that these students either do not want to work hard or have very low skills, often both. Class size is rarely adjusted for this impossibly hard task, so one year I had twenty-eight juniors and seniors packed into a portable classroom behind the school. All but two were young men, and 40 percent of them had failed the course the year before. Worse, the curriculum was not adjusted either. I struggled to bridge the vocabulary and context of *The Great Gatsby* for these students, but there were no miracles that year. In fact, that class taught me instead. Every time I tuned out what was expected of me by my department chair and tuned into what I knew my students needed, things improved. Aaron went from setting off the fire alarm in seven-below-zero weather one February to researching the art and science of scarification. My regret is how often I turned back to our American literature curriculum. It fit on two pages: a list of books and a list of punctuation skills. There was no deep thinking there, but I followed it. The very idea haunts me.

If Crystal had come to me a dozen years before she did, when I was just starting to assemble a few books for my classroom library, it is unlikely she would have read fifty-two books. When class sizes still crested above thirty and I didn't understand how well a reading and writing workshop could challenge and support high school students, I saw few leaps in understanding. I saw few miracles.

Last year I was poised to help this girl—but first I had to confront my own unwillingness to meet kids where they are. Picture this: two weeks of work in notebooks and studying mentor texts (or rather, I passed them out and tried to engage reluctant readers in noticing how they worked), conferences on ideas, encouragement, more encouragement, and then, on the day it was due—*it* being the carefully revised and edited masterpiece crafted over time that I expected—Crystal handed me pages from her notebook (see Figures 1 and 2).

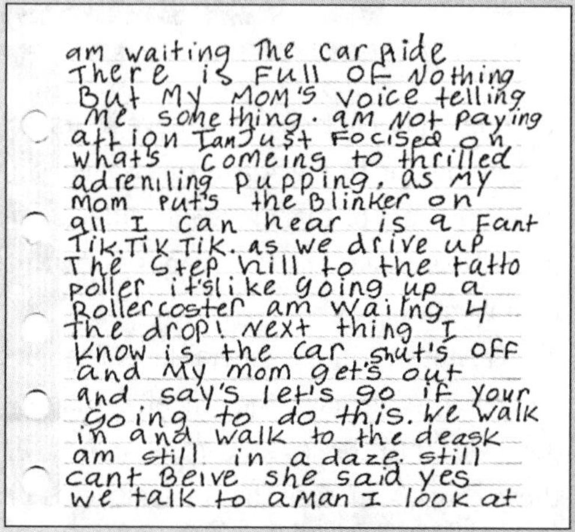
am waiting The car Ride
There is Full OF Nothing
But My MOM'S voice telling
Me something. am Not paying
attion IanJust Focised on
what's comeing to thrilled
adreniling pupping, as My
Mom put's the Blinker on
all I can hear is a Fant
Tik.Tik Tik. as we drive up
The Step hill to the tatto
poller it'slike going up a
Rollercoster am Wailng 4
the drop! Next thing I
Know is the car shut's OFF
and My mom get's out
and say's let's go if your
going to do this. We walk
in and walk to the deask
am still in a daze. still
cant Beive she said yes
we talk to aMan I look at

Figure 1 *Crystal's notebook page*

Time out for the silent scream.

I know we must start where they are, but does that mean here? Don Graves would say, in his calm, generous voice, "Every kid has a story." He didn't mean Crystal's trip to the tattoo parlor, either. I could hear my snarky response: *Not now, my grades are due*. I reached for the dark chocolate.

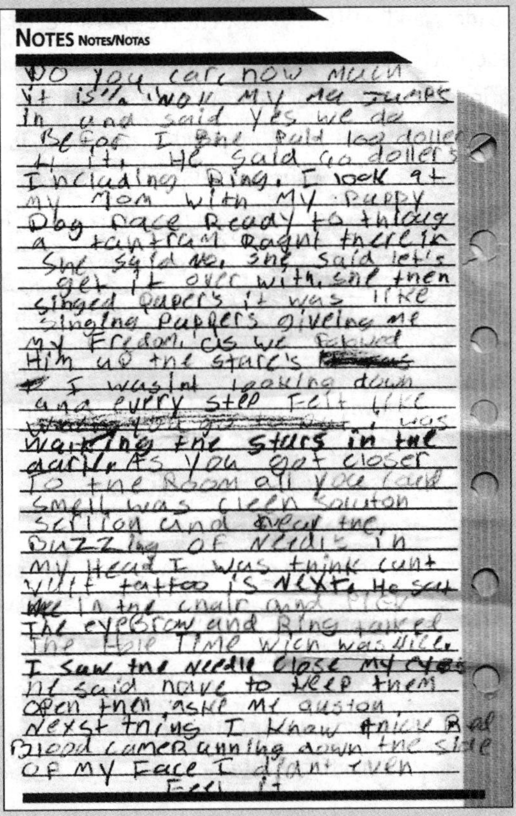

I moved her draft to the bottom of the stack as I sat on my couch that Sunday night. I stomped my feet a bit. When I finally faced her writing, I had to slow down. Stop. Read her words. Think about her intentions as a writer. Think about her deficits and what to address first. I couldn't grade this, not if I wanted a chance with her. My principal expects my grades to be updated every two weeks, and my department chair monitors them, but sometimes I can't deliver. Crystal needed feedback, not evaluation. She needed to use this essay as a starting point, work from there to gather skills and understanding, and in doing so accumulate a portfolio she could hand me in June that showed improvement. It was possible. I just couldn't see it yet. I saw all toil and no harvest in the months ahead.

I went in the next day and told her I couldn't grade her work until she spent time revising. I began teaching her. She tried. Not every day, but most days. She told me *if* she made it to June she would be the first in all the generations of her family to finish high school. I wanted to help her. I believe Crystal trusted me because I was standing on the shoulders of my colleagues who had carried her through horrors she endured in the years before she came to my class. She could have walked away in ninth grade when nocturnal seizures kept her up all night and absences accumulated. She could have dropped out many times, but there was a warrior inside her fighting for more.

Figure 2 *Crystal's notebook page*

This was a tough class, though. It is always challenging to build a community of readers and writers. It is delicate work. Yet students will learn more as they listen to each other and work together. It has to be a priority. In this class many students were grieving. We had lost two boys in car accidents the previous July. When we studied writing in an editorial entitled "Cruel as It Is, We Somehow Go On" by Leonard Pitts Jr., my students were feeling the cruelties of living and all wrote of loss in their notebooks. I collected student imitations of Pitts' writing that day, then we revised together to create this:

> Sometimes, life is cruel.
>
>   A caring volunteer firefighter, just 17, on his way home from babysitting with his girlfriend, falls asleep, drifts into a tree, and never wakes up.
>
>   Sometimes, life is cruel.
>
>   Kids out being kids on a summer's night, lose control of the car and spend the next week caught between a funeral, gathering at the site of the accident, or at the hospital waiting for one boy to wake up from a coma.
>
>   Sometimes life is cruel and when it is, we do what we always do: we call; we question; we cry; we pray; we remember the good times; we draw close to our friends; we go on.
>
>   Sometimes, life is cruel.

I could feel a shift in our classroom community after this. We had a sense of purpose. The poster of their words hung in my classroom all year, acting like an adhesive to bind us to each other and to the work in reading and writing that each of us needed to do.

The turning point in my work with Crystal came from a novel, *Bitter End*, by Jennifer Brown. It tells the story of a girl whose boyfriend hits her, but as I explained in my book talk, because he is so good to her when he isn't hitting her, I finally began to understand why a girl might stay. Violence accelerates, though, and this book leads you to hard places, I told the class. Crystal asked for the book.

She was at my door the next morning at 6:30. "Mrs. Kittle," she said, "I need another book like this one." I told her I didn't know of another one. She interrupted me, "I stayed up all night reading. I want another story like this one." I couldn't help her, so she read it again. She read it three times. The novel gave Crystal a vision for her own story, a story she needed to make sense of. She approached this writing with tenacity and insight.

Crystal read three dozen works of fiction senior year. She said, "I've always been a good reader, but this year I made a better reading habit, so good that I can't put the book down until I finish. My habit is to read until I get so tired I can't keep my eyes open." In fourth quarter alone she read fifteen novels, from *The Lovely Bones*, by Alice Sebold, to *The Sweet Hereafter*, by Russell Banks. She also read a biography, a play, and Wally Lamb's *Couldn't Keep It to Myself*, a series of life stories written by women prisoners. Her final reading list included six genres.

The books gave her courage to write her story. I've grown weary of those who think story is a lesser genre. If you imagine story is easy to write, that it doesn't require all your skills to reason and organize and skillfully design sentences, then you probably haven't written one that tells your heart. At some point in the year most students have said something to me like Jacob did third quarter when he tried to write about his track coach: "This is too hard!"—each hand clutching a fistful of hair—"Will you just give me one of those essays to write instead?" I laughed. "No, seriously," he glared, "I'll write two of those instead of this."

We find our stories in our notebooks. Crystal wrote furiously in hers, pages and pages in blood-red ink. One morning she asked to see me in the hall. "I want to read you something." We stood alone outside the door. She hesitated and looked at her feet. Her eyes were full when she glanced back at me and said, "I don't want you to judge me."

"I won't," I said.

She looked at her words, clutching her notebook with both hands.

It was a moment built on a thousand others. Would she trust me? She had constructed a profile of me that included my most vulnerable moments. She listened and watched me in class, on hall and lunch duty. We are always on display in school. Everything matters. I know that writing in front of her class about what has been most difficult in my life created a bridge for her, but still she hesitated. "Everyone says I should have never let this happen"—she started, then exhaled—"I just need you to listen."

"Okay," I said.

She began reading:

> He told me to come and sit on his lap so I did. The next thing I knew I
> was being punched in the stomach repeatedly over and over. I didn't cry.
> I held them back; I just leaned into him. As I did he whispered, "That's
> my trooper." Within thirty seconds he realized what he had done. He
> then held on to me and apologized to me. Then it was time to go. We
> were expected for a cookout at my brother's house, which was planned

for weeks. As we got there I felt sick and crampy. He acted as if there
was nothing wrong. As I started to cook I almost fell over and dropped
the food.

The details of her miscarriage and continued abuse by a boyfriend halted time
that morning. Here was her life, the one hidden beneath the draft written in colored
pencil from October.

I said only, "Crystal, I'm so sorry." We heard footsteps coming down the hall, the
only sound on this still Wednesday morning. "You are brave to write this. It was one
thing to live it—but writing makes you live it again."

She nodded. "So it's okay?"

"Yes; keep writing if you can"—I hesitated, waiting for the student to pass,
bathroom pass in hand—"but I have to ask you two things. Are you safe now?"

"Yes. He moved to Mass. There was a trial. It'll all be in my piece."

"Okay." I hesitated. "But I'm curious—who are you writing this for?"

At first she said she didn't know—then she said for herself—and then just as I
put my hand on the doorknob she said, "I actually think if this could help someone
else, I'd like that." I nodded. "Like this girl in my dance class fourth period." I let go
of the door.

She told me how a freshman had come to class breathless the day before. Crystal
asked her if she was worried about being late. She said no, her boyfriend likes to pick
her up and slam her against the wall so he can hear the air rush out of her chest. He
likes that sound, she repeated. He does this in a hall away from cameras and monitors,
so the adults in the school haven't seen it. He laughs afterward so the kids walking by
just keep going, but Crystal said, "I'm worried about her."

I'm stunned by what we don't know.

I've always believed writing about what matters is not just for the writer. When
we name the conflicts in our lives, we open the door for others. As Franz Kafka said,
"A book must be the ax for the frozen sea within us." And then, "If the book we are
reading does not wake us, as with a fist hammering on our skulls, then why do we read
it? Good God, we also would be happy if we had no books . . . we could, if need be,
write ourselves." And there was Crystal—writing for herself and for a girl she hardly
knows. I assured her I would go to the dance teacher at lunch and we would find help.
But there are surely others in my school and in yours. How do we find them?

Transcribing the draft from her writing notebook to a computer was laborious.
Crystal still wrote in her notebook without paragraphs or punctuation and with abysmal

spelling. She still drafted from emotion and without punctuation. When a story must be told, however, students have shown me again and again that they'll put the time in, hours beyond what we assign them, hours of practice rereading and revising that changes everything. Crystal did. Her draft became seven single-spaced typed pages. She would be at my door when I arrived at 6:30, her hair wet, eyes droopy, but ready to revise. I would listen as she read her work aloud, sentence by sentence, so that she could decide what punctuation was needed to help a reader.

Crystal called this editing process "adding voice," which was odd to me, but it made sense if you sat beside us on those mornings. She read aloud, stopping to say, "I need a pause here," then inserting a comma or a period, finally having a use for language she'd heard teachers use for years. "This is a full stop: period." Then she would reread and sometimes ask me, "Is that right?" She needed my help because she didn't trust herself to know yet. And this was her last piece of writing, finished days before graduation, so of course I worry about that. Who will help her in college? It isn't right that she's not ready.

Crystal had lots of one kind of help in school. Most of her papers came back with corrections. But what good are a teacher's corrections? In my June interview with her, Crystal said, "If they just put like a dot here—a semicolon there—then it's like in my next piece; how am I supposed to know where it goes? Mostly when teachers correct you, they're just like 'okay, do this next time' and if not, they're going to correct you again, so they just keep correcting you over and over instead of giving you the chance to do it yourself." Why does this happen? Because teachers in public high schools are given hundreds of kids to teach at once, and reading hundreds of rough drafts poses an impossible trade—time with family or five hours of reading this weekend? Sometimes we correct errors and call it teaching. It isn't.

What helped Crystal were her conferences with me about a piece of writing she cared enough to read and reread in order to improve it. She described it like this, "I think I learned right around when I wrote the story about my brother, the rosary beads one, and it just kept running on and on and on, and I stopped and said, 'Wait, this doesn't make sense,' and then I finally started putting in periods and commas and you came over and were like, 'That's good, that's where it's supposed to go, keep doing it,' and you'd start making me do it on my own instead of you just doing it, and then you'd look it over and help me with the ones I missed."

I asked her if she thought her reading had helped her understand punctuation better. She said, "It did—especially the stories I read—some of them had a lot of run-on sentences but that's because like people were talking and so there are purposes sometimes for run-on sentences and there are times when you need to stop and take a breath." Crystal didn't just read a little, she read, as Gary Paulsen said, "like a wolf eats" (see photo).

I want you crouched on the floor of the gym with me as we watch her rise with

her class and make her way to the podium on a perfect June morning. Generations of her family walked the halls of our school, then walked out. Crystal stayed.

I loved the moment when she turned toward me, diploma in hand, a head nod in recognition. But there was more. The principal called her name moments later as the most improved student in the senior class. A thousand guests slowly rose in a standing ovation. Twelve members of her family stood. Every member of the senior class stood. I have her proud grin on film, but the video wobbles as I crouch there, balancing on heels, willing myself to steady my hands, soak this in, and stop crying. The harvest comes.

Crystal's deep reading in our year together changed her.

Books changed her.

Writing changed her.

What I know for sure: from this moment on, I am not the teacher I was last September. Crystal changed me.

Dreams lurk in books. We must never forget that. We have been given the privilege of this life in teaching. Let us have the strength to start where they are and lead them.

The Book Love Foundation

(www.booklovefoundation.org)

Istood in a most wonderful bookstore in the Memphis airport one evening inhaling the strong scent of Bar-B-Q that permeates the place. On maple bookshelves softly lit by spotlights, I came upon a collection of animal books, not just *The Art of Racing in the Rain*, by Garth Stein, and *A Dog's Purpose*, by Bruce Cameron, but *Cassius: The True Story of a Courageous Police Dog*, by Gordon Thorburn, which explores the scenting capabilities of police dogs that help solve crimes. There were books about training birds, the history of zoos, and endangered species. I thought of current students who would enjoy each title. This intriguing collection was placed directly across from classics recommended by people who worked in the store. There was a shelf of new fiction, one of psychology and self-discovery, and a section for business books. The store went on and on. You know: a book for anyone who might wander through this place. It was hard not to pick them up, hard not to stuff my suitcase even fuller. (I did, in fact.) But I also twirled around the room for a moment and imagined clearing out the center shelves in the store and putting in tables, writing notebooks, and students. Every classroom should have a similar celebration of reading. We need books for every reader, recommended by readers, shelved by interests, inviting browsing.

When I speak to teachers about leading readers, they want a place like this, and I want it for them. Many contact me after bargaining with their principals and colleagues to set up classroom libraries and support independent reading. Jason BreMiller wrote, "I was skeptical at first at the thought of my students really digging deep to explore books and to create their own reading lives. But what I've found, to my great happiness, is that they have; they do. The bulk of my students have thrown themselves into their independent reading projects with verve, as if they've been waiting for this opportunity all along. For many, it's returned them to a time in their lives when the simple power and joy of stories was alive for them. They give book talks and listen attentively to each others' reading experiences. They write reflectively about how their books move them. Freed from the imposition of having to read books they haven't chosen, they bring a refreshing bout of honesty to their thoughts about these books. Mostly, though, they've read books—a cause for celebration both amongst the students and their growing list of texts-finished, and for me, their teacher, who has observed from afar the unconscious, often subtle (but clear-as-day!) literacy benefits they've made by reading more than they have ever read before. Many of my students consider themselves readers now and have built a momentum that will propel them into a life of reading." Kristina wrote, "I left your [UNH summer school] class armed with great ideas and a ton of passion and shared it all with my principal, who gave me $300 for books. With that, a lot of my own money, and a ton of book suggestions from you, I created a classroom library. It's no surprise that my kids are reading like crazy. Even my study hall kids who see the books are taking advantage of them. Recently, two other teachers decided to jump on board. Armed with my reading rate charts and student essays, we approached our principal, who agreed to give us EACH a THOUSAND dollars toward a classroom library for next year!"

My heart expands with stories like these.

But the truth is, as budgets have shrunk, books and libraries and school librarians have been cut in far too many schools. Books can have an incredible effect on children's lives, yet there's only one book for every three hundred kids living in poverty in the U.S. (Reading Is Fundamental). I believe every child in America needs access to books that will keep him or her turning pages, racing to the end, discovering new ideas, and learning to understand the diversity in our world. I believe all children deserve books they can and will want to read and teachers that will guide them to improve as readers. We need access to books from every corner of the world and from every field of study. Students should have access to all the current award winners in literature and to the wide range of genres they will read in the future. Every classroom should have hundreds of books to inspire curiosity, hope, and vision for the future.

So here's what I'm working on. It's called the Book Love Foundation (www.book lovefoundation.org), a nonprofit organization with one goal: to put books in the hands of teachers of teenagers. My husband and I will raise as much money as we can to fund starter classroom libraries of five hundred books each. We seek passionately committed teachers who will aim instruction toward increasing volume, stamina, and joy in reading in middle and high school. Each year the board of directors will fund as many libraries as we can. Heinemann has generously agreed to fund one set a year, and so will Pat and I. I will be begging for money everywhere I go, so if you know anyone who loves reading and wants to help teachers, let them know about this foundation.

We can change the story of reading.

We have to.

Every child. Every year. Every classroom.

Book love—pass it on.

Works Cited

Allen, Patrick A. 2009. *Conferring: The Keystone of Reader's Workshop*. Portland, ME: Stenhouse.

Allington, Richard L. 2001. *What Really Matters for Struggling Readers*. Boston: Addison Wesley Longman.

———. 2009. *What Really Matters in Fluency*. Boston: Allyn & Bacon.

———. 2012. "Summer: Some Are Reading, Some Are Not." Speech presented at the Colorado Council of the International Reading Association annual meeting, Denver, Colorado, February 3.

Anderson, Carl. 2000. *How's It Going?* Portsmouth, NH: Heinemann.

Anderson, Jeff. 2005. *Mechanically Inclined*. Portland, ME: Stenhouse.

———. 2007. *Everyday Editing*. Portland, ME: Stenhouse.

———. 2011. *Ten Things Every Writer Needs to Know*. Portland, ME: Stenhouse.

Anderson, Laurie Halse. 2009. *Wintergirls*. New York: Viking Juvenile.

Anderson, R. C., P. T. Wilson, and L. G. Fielding. 1988. "Growth in Reading and How Children Spend Their Time Outside of School." *Reading Research Quarterly* 23: 285–303.

Atwell, Nancie. 1988. *In the Middle*. Portsmouth, NH: Heinemann.

———. 2007. *The Reading Zone*. New York: Scholastic.

———. 2009. *Atwell Rebuttal*. Video. Available at www.heinemann.com/shared/player .aspx?id=AtwellRebuttal&path=rtmp://heinpublishing.flashsvc.vitalstreamcdn.com/ heinpublishing_vitalstream_com/_definst_/videos/atwell. Accessed 7/22/12.

Ballard, Chris. 2010. *The Art of a Beautiful Game*. New York: Simon & Schuster.

Bauerlein, Mark. 2008. "Screen No Match for the Page in Education." *The Australian News,* October 24. Available at www.theaustralian.com.au/screen-no-match-for-the-page/story-fna7dq6e-1111117688867.

Beers, Kylene. 2011. Boothbay Literacy Retreat, Boothbay, Maine, June 26–29.

Bennett, Samantha. 2011. "How to Choose a Just Right Book." Available at www .literacylabs.org, September 23. Accessed 04/11/2012.

Bowen, William, Matthew M. Chingos, and Michael McPherson. 2011. *Crossing the Finish Line: Completing College at America's Public Universities.* Princeton: Princeton University Press.

Broz, William J. 2011. "Not Reading: The 800-Pound Mockingbird in the Classroom." *English Journal* 100 (5): 15.

Carr, Nicholas. 2010. *The Shallows: What the Internet Is Doing to Our Brains.* Boston: W. W. Norton.

Clark, Christina, and Kate Rumbold. 2006. "Reading for Pleasure: A Research Overview." London: National Literacy Trust. Available at www.scholastic.com.

Cleave, Christopher. 2010. *Little Bee.* New York: Simon & Schuster.

Collins, Suzanne. 2009. *Catching Fire.* New York: Scholastic.

Daniels, Harvey, Steven Zemelman, and Nancy Steineke. 2007. *Content-Area Writing.* Portsmouth, NH: Heinemann.

Dutton, Dennis. 2009. *The Art Instinct: Beauty, Pleasure, and Human Evolution.* London: Oxford University Press.

Education Quality and Accountability Office (EQAO). 2011. "EQAO Assessment of Reading, Writing, and Mathematics, Primary Division (Grades 1–3)." Toronto: Education Quality and Accountability Office.

Forman, Gayle. 2009. *If I Stay.* New York: Dutton Juvenille.

Gallagher, Kelly. 2009. *Readicide.* Portland, ME: Stenhouse.

———. 2011. *Write Like This.* Portland, ME: Stenhouse.

Gioia, Dana. 2007. "To Read or Not to Read: A Question of National Consequence." Washington, DC: National Endowment for the Arts.

Gladwell, Malcolm. 2008. *Outliers: The Story of Success.* Boston: Little, Brown.

Gordon, Carol, and Ya-Ling Lu. 2007. "'I Hate to Read—or Do I?' Low Achievers and Their Reading." Available at www.ala.org/ala/mgrps/divs/aasl/aaslpubsandjournals/slmrb/slmrcontents/volume11/gordon_lu.cfm.

Graham, Steve, and Dolores Perin. 2007. "Writing Next: Effective Strategies to Improve Writing of Adolescents in Middle and High School." A report to the Carnegie Corporation of New York. New York: Carnegie Corporation.

Graves, Donald H. 1983/2003. *Writing: Teachers and Children at Work.* Portsmouth, NH: Heinemann.

Graves, Donald H., and Penny Kittle. 2005. *Inside Writing: How to Teach the Details of Craft.* Portsmouth, NH: Heinemann.

Grossman, Lev. 2008. "Outliers: Malcolm Gladwell's Success Story." *Time*, November 13.

Handler, Daniel, and Maria Kalman. 2011. *Why We Broke Up.* Boston: Little, Brown.

Hopkins, Ellen. 2012. "What Should Kids Be Reading?" In *What Kids Are Reading: The Book-Reading Habits of Students in American Schools*, 59. Wisconsin Rapids, WI: Renaissance Learning.

Jacobs, Allan. 2011. *The Pleasures of Reading in an Age of Distraction.* New York: Oxford University Press.

Johnston, Peter. 2004. *Choice Words.* Portland, ME: Stenhouse.

———. 2012. *Opening Minds.* Portland, ME: Stenhouse.

Kaiser Foundation. 2010. *Generation M2: Media in the Lives of 8-to-18-Year-Olds.* Menlo Park, CA: Henry J. Kaiser Family Foundation.

Kittle, Penny. 2008. *Write Beside Them.* Portsmouth, NH: Heinemann.

Kohn, Alfie. 1993. *Punished by Rewards.* Boston: Houghton Mifflin Harcourt.

Krashen, Stephen. 1993. *The Power of Reading.* Santa Barbara, CA: Libraries Unlimited.

Lesesne, Teri. 2010. *Reading Ladders.* Portsmouth, NH: Heinemann.

Marzano, Robert, Debra Pickering, and Jane Pollock. 2001. *Classroom Instruction That Works.* Alexandria, VA: Association for Supervision and Curriculum Development (ASCD).

Millen, Elaine. 2010. Personal interview, October 18.

Miller, Donalyn. 2009. *The Book Whisperer.* San Francisco: Jossey-Bass.

———. 2012. Keynote address at the Colorado Council of the International Reading Association annual meeting, Denver, Colorado, February 3.

Morgan, Paul L., and Douglas Fuchs. 2007. "Is There a Bidirectional Relationship Between Children's Reading Skills and Reading Motivation?" *Exceptional Children* 73 (2): 165–83.

Murray, Donald M. 1993. *Read to Write.* 3d ed. New York: Harcourt Brace Jovanovich.

National Center on Education and the Economy. 2007. *Tough Choices or Tough Times.* Washington, DC: National Center on Education and the Economy.

National Endowment for the Arts (NEA). 2007. "To Read or Not to Read: A Question of National Consequence." Executive summary. Washington, DC: National Endowment for the Arts.

Newkirk, Thomas. 2011. *The Art of Slow Reading.* Portsmouth, NH: Heinemann.

Patchett, Ann. 2009. "The Triumph of the Readers." *Wall Street Journal*, January 23.

People for Education. 2011. "Reading for Joy." Toronto: People for Education. Available at www.accessola.org/ola_dev/Documents/OLA/issues/Reading-for-Joy.pdf.

Pilkey, Dav. 2012. "What Should Kids Be Reading?" In *What Kids Are Reading: The Book-Reading Habits of Students in American Schools*, 28. Wisconsin Rapids, WI: Renaissance Learning.

Pruzinsky, Timothy. 2012. Personal interview, January 25.

Quirk, M. P., and P. J. Schwanenflugel. 2004. "Do Supplemental Remedial Reading Programs Address the Motivational Issues of Struggling Readers? An Analysis of Five Popular Programs." *Reading Research and Instruction* 43: 1–19.

Ray, Katie Wood. 1999. *Wondrous Words.* Urbana, IL: National Council of Teachers of English.

Reading Is Fundamental (RIF). Available at www.rif.org. Accessed 7/16/12.

Reeves, Douglas B. 2004. "The Case Against the Zero." *Phi Delta Kappan* 86 (4): 324–25.

Renaissance Learning, Inc. 2012. *What Kids Are Reading: The Book-Reading Habits of Students in American Schools.* Wisconsin Rapids, WI: Renaissance Learning.

Rief, Linda. 1991. *Seeking Diversity.* Portsmouth, NH: Heinemann.

———. 2003. *100 Quickwrites: Fast and Effective Freewriting Exercises That Build Students' Confidence, Develop Their Fluency, and Bring Out the Writer in Every Student.* New York: Scholastic.

———. 2007. *Inside the Writer's–Reader's Notebook.* Portsmouth, NH: Heinemann.

Rosenblatt, Louise M. 1976. *Literature as Exploration.* New York: Noble and Noble.

Rosenthal, Amy Krouse. 2005. *Encyclopedia of an Ordinary Life.* New York: Random House/Three Rivers Press.

"Sample Performance Task." Council for Aid to Education Collegiate Learning Assessment (CLA). Available at www.cae.org/content/pro_collegiate_sample_measures.htm. Accessed 7/22/12.

Schlafly, Phyllis. 2007. "Advice to College Students: Don't Major in English." *Human Events* (online publication), October 1. Available at www.humanevents .com/2007/10/01/advice-to-college-students-dont-major-in-english/.

Society for American Baseball Research. n.d. "Baseball's Triple Plays (1876–Present)." Available at http://tripleplays.sabr.org. Accessed 7/22/12.

Spear-Swerling, L., and R. J. Sternberg. 1994. "The Road Not Taken: An Integrative Theoretical Model of Reading Disability." *Journal of Learning Disabilities* 27: 91–103.

Stanovich, Keith E. 1986. "Matthew Effects in Reading: Some Consequences of Individual Differences in the Acquisition of Literacy." *Reading Research Quarterly* 21 (4): 360–40.

Strommen, L., and B. Mates. 2004. "Learning to Love Reading: Interviews with Older Children and Teens." *Journal of Adolescent and Adult Literacy* 48: 188–200.

Trelease, Jim. 2006. *The Read-Aloud Handbook*. New York: Penguin.

Tovani, Cris. 2011. *So What Do They Really Know?* Portsmouth, NH: Heinemann.

Ulin, David L. 2010. *The Lost Art of Reading: Why Books Matter in a Distracted Time*. Seattle: Sasquatch.

Willingham, Daniel T. 2009. *Why Don't Students Like School? A Cognitive Scientist Answers Questions About How the Mind Works and What It Means for the Classroom*. San Francisco: Jossey-Bass.

Wilson, Maja. 2006. *Rethinking Rubrics*. Portsmouth, NH: Heinemann.

Woodrell, Daniel. 2007. *Winter's Bone*. Boston: Back Bay Books.

Zimmermann, Susan, and Chryse Hutchins. 2003. *7 Keys to Comprehension: How to Help Your Kids Read It and Get It!* New York: Random House/Three Rivers Press.